VACATION HOME

Photo courtesy Town & Country Cedar Homes

The Complete Guide to Planning and Building

RICH BINSACCA

HOME PLANNERS, LLC
Wholly owned by Hanley-Wood, LLC
TTUCSON, ARIZONA

International Standard Book Number: 1-881955-86-9
Library of Congress Catalog Card Number: 00-110253
Home Planners, LLC
Wholly owned by Hanley-Wood, LLC
Tucson, Arizona 85741

10 9 8 7 6 5 4 3 2 1

Book design by Paul Fitzgerald
Cover photos: Top left: Courtesy Town & Country Cedar Homes (also shown on title page)
Top Right: Vacation Plan DSA055; photo by Oscar Thompson Photography. For more information about this plan, call 1-800-521-6797.

Bottom Middle: Vacation Plan HPB920; Photo by Bob Greenspan. For more information about this plan, call 1-800-521-6797.

Dedication

This book is dedicated to my parents, Bob and Lynn; to my two sons, Sam and Nick; to Duanea; and to my friend Gerry Donohue, who inspired the idea.

Acknowledgements

This book would not have been possible without the extreme patience, excellent editing and overall management skill of Paulette Mulvin at Home Planners, LLC, as well as the talents of graphic designer Paul Fitzgerald.

I owe thanks to several folks who contributed their time, expertise, professional skill and general support to this project (whether they knew it or not) including: Bill Klimback; Gerry Donohue; Sarah Dvir; Betsy McFadden, Kevin McKee, Mike Hahn and the staff at Kevin McKee Associates architects; Melissa Dole; Laurie and Mark Anderson,; Charles and Dee Williams; Jamie Williams and Carol Lieske; the American Resort Development Association; and the National Association of Home Builders.

Many of the photographs appearing in this book were contributed free of charge by several companies and photographers. Special thanks to Town & Country Cedar Homes; Precision Craft Log Structures, Bob Franzese, Photographer; Hearthstone Homes; Trus Joist; Classic Post & Beam, Lok-N-Logs; The Wilderness Company/Geneva Log Homes; Northeastern Log Homes; Ward Log Homes; James F. Wilson, Photographer; Jason Monroe/Idaho Truss; CertainTeed; Style Solutions; Ideal Homes; Welsh Studio; Pirozzolo Company Public Relations; Brad Simmons; Pella Windows; and Home Planners, LLC.

And, of course, I should acknowledge the hundreds of builders, subcontractors, architects, real estate journalists and building products representatives, among others in this industry whom I've met during the last 13 or so years. Their insight and enthusiasm have helped me build a body of knowledge and perspective about the home building industry without which the production of this book would not have been possible.

Photo by Rich Binsacca

CONTENTS

PREFACE

A vacation home is about relaxation and getting away from it all, even for a just a weekend.

I learned to drive a stick shift on vacation. Specifically, a five-speed, 1984 Honda Accord hatchback on the winding roads of Sea Ranch, a sprawling development of shingle-sided vacation homes along the Northern California coast.

It happened during a week with my family at one of those oceanside cottages. Despite months of frustration trying to master the complexities of a clutch, I was allowed to take the car one morning to play golf and, I suppose, learn how to drive it out of pure necessity.

After gulping and sputtering out of the driveway in typical fashion, however, I hit my stride on the access road, then made a successful entrance onto the main highway. The tensions of the past vanished; my driving was relaxed, my shifting smooth. Like a kid who has gained his balance on a bicycle for the first time, I had crossed over and forever into the world of standard transmissions.

Looking back, and thinking about this book, I credit the context of my situation for my success that morning. Logically and physically, I knew the basic operation of a clutch; mentally, I had been blocked by the stresses of a parent in the passenger seat and of driving around my neighborhood. The comforts of home, I guess, had actually become a burden.

But at Sea Ranch, I was relaxed. I love the ocean, anyway, so I already had achieved a measure of peace before I climbed behind the wheel. And there were no lines on the access road, much less other vehicles pressing in behind me—and I was alone in the car. Being away from the paralyzingly familiar had loosened me up ... and allowed me to properly focus on the task at hand.

I have since found that other vacations also allowed me to refocus and think more clearly. It doesn't typically take very long. Rather, it requires only a short break from the routine, a silencing of the white noise of an everyday existence, even for just a few days. And, for me and perhaps most folks in today's working world, being able to flop on a couch and read all day, take a nap after lunch, eat dinner at nine-thirty (and breakfast whenever)—to mention just a few simple pleasures—underscores the true value of a vacation home.

The middle-class suburb east of San Francisco where I grew up offered the opportunity to enjoy a variety of vacation options within a reasonable driving distance. Sea Ranch, for instance, where we occasionally rented the vacation home of a family friend, was about three hours away, as was Lake Tahoe to the east, toward the Sierra Nevada mountains. We rented houses there, too, from a rustic log cabin along the lakeshore to a more polished condo with a manicured landscape and tennis court. Those days are some of my most vivid vacation memories.

Vacations allow me to refocus and think more clearly .

I live in Boise, Idaho now. The Pacific Ocean is a long drive or, more likely, a plane ride and another hour's drive away, and thus a rare vacation spot for me anymore. But Idaho has spectacular mountains, wild rivers and alpine lakes. Within a few hours' drive is the resort and vacation mecca of Sun Valley and, for more rustic types, the towns of Stanley and Garden Valley, among several others along the Salmon and Snake rivers. For the most part, Boiseans make up the vacation and seasonal homeowners of those places, providing the essence of vacation—the need (and ability) to simply get away from the city for a long weekend or perhaps a whole week.

Such a lifestyle is heaven to some and a colossal bore to others who prefer to travel and experience different cultures on their vacation time. While those folks may purchase a timeshare or even arrange a house swap in a faraway place, the process and permanence of building a sec-

No matter the setting— ocean, lake, or mountains—a vacation home is your retreat.

ond or vacation home is outside their comfort zone. But for the majority of people with the means and time to do so, vacation homes are among the most desirable by-products of professional success, providing a respite for today's stressed-out, career-focused work force.

This book is for those people who envision themselves as I do someday—lounging on a covered porch in an Adirondack chair with a cool beverage, watching the sunset behind the far reaches of the ocean, distanced physically and mentally from my cares and concerns.

INTRODUCTION: BOOM TIMES

The number of vacation homes is expected to grow to nearly 10 million this decade.

That sonic boom you're about to hear is the vast number of people in their late forties and fifties, and a fair share of younger beneficiaries of the so-called "new economy," beginning construction on their second homes. No longer exemplified by the vacation villas of the rich, vacation and second homes are perched on the edge of the mainstream as increased wealth among more people propels the market.

Sure, you still need some measure of discretionary income and savings, or at least enough stock options to leverage a land purchase and another mortgage, to afford your own home away from home. But as the bulk of the 80-million-plus population of the baby-boom generation matures into its peak earning years, joined by a group of successful (often younger) entrepreneurs from high-tech industries, demand for what

This book is designed to be a realistic and honest approach to building a second home.

American Demographics magazine found to be the number-one symbol of success—owning a second home—is expected to increase 40 percent through the current decade and into the next.

That's a pretty lofty statistic considering history. Fewer than 7 million second or vacation homes exist in the U.S., representing a small fraction of the 110 million or so homes currently standing coast to coast. But several factors beyond sheer demographics of our nation's largest-ever generation are pushing the market for vacation and second homes.

Coupled with increased demand by more people with more money looking for a little stress relief is a shrinking supply of available, desirable land for vacation and second homes. Regardless of your political or

Rural settings and finishes, such as log homes and cabins, are a popular vacation home style.

economic stance on land-use rights, the fact is that some of the most likely locations for new second and vacation homes are being cordoned off like museum displays, for viewing only.

> *The value of a vacation home is almost priceless.*

Another, if less tangible, driver of the second- and vacation-home market is our need to simply relax. Today's vacation-home price tags may seem like a hefty sum to pay for lemonade on a porch swing, but the flip side—that of creating a weekend retreat and avoiding the hassles of airports and traveler's checks, language barriers and misplaced reservations—is arguably an equal trade-off. In fact, I'd say the value of a vacation home is almost priceless.

Vacation versus Travel

Essentially, a second home exemplifies the difference between "vacation" and "travel," in defining the type of sanctuary the vast majority of us seek. The former implies an opportunity to get away from the routines of everyday life, from work and taxes, from the rules of practicality and functionality.

Travel, by some contrast, indicates (and often demands) disciplines of planning, scheduling and meeting deadlines, if in simply a different place than where you live and work. You may travel to a vacation destination, but very few of us can truly travel as a form of vacation and reap the same benefits of relaxation and sensory decompression afforded by a second home.

There are other priorities and qualities to consider, of course, including whether you even have the personality to enjoy, much less be involved in the design and construction of a vacation home. In addition to a trilogy of primary considerations (outlined in Chapter 1), a second home may someday be where you retire, serve as a family gathering place, or perhaps generate a secondary income. All of these and other factors will drive your decisions regarding where your second home will be and what form it will take.

Setting the Stage

This book is about vacation homes and, synonymously, second homes. Commonly, these terms are kept separate to differentiate their intended uses. A "vacation" home, for instance, suggests an occasional getaway, while a "second" home implies a longer period of time, perhaps an entire season, spent in the house.

In this context, however, the two terms are interchangeable. Both cer-

Creating your own vacation spot, in both style and function, is one of the pleasures of building a second home.

tainly are different than timeshares and house-swapping clubs, resort complexes and even owner-occupied condominiums.

Unlike those options, vacation homes are stand-alone (or detached) single-family houses, designed, built for and used by their owners. They are fully functional dwellings, with no shared areas or services, intended primarily (and often solely) to be a home away from home for a particular person, couple or family.

This somewhat narrower definition of second homes is in response to how most people envision a vacation retreat. In periodic surveys conducted for the American Resort Development Association since 1990, and more recently in 1999, a single-family vacation home or cabin is what most folks say they're interested in purchasing within the next ten years. Owning a vacant lot (presumably on which to eventually build a vacation home) is the second most popular choice.

Building a second home, however, is the most complex option for creating a vacation getaway, requiring a significant time and financial commitment, as well as a solid understanding of the process. There's no mystery or real work involved in buying (much less renting) a pre-designed condo or timeshare. Creating your ideal getaway, from initial concept through land purchasing and construction, is a different and far more intensive undertaking. The payoffs, though, outweigh the work.

Building the Ideal Getaway

That work starts with setting priorities and sticking with them in the face of challenges from secondary considerations. If your goal is to create a personal retreat that is easily accessible, readily available and offers the least amount of hassle and compromise, you'll need to fight off the urge to stray from the trio of primary considerations outlined in Chapter 1.

Next is defining yourself, creating a Lifestyle Profile that will help shape what you need and want from a vacation home, from its general location (or setting) to the initial concept of its physical design and layout. For years, whether you realize it or not, you've been storing information and images about your ideal vacation home. The process for bringing out those memories and transforming them into an articulate, if still rough, concept is presented in Chapter 2. It's also a chance to figure out if, indeed, a second home is the most appropriate vacation option for your lifestyle.

Your involvement throughout the process, even during construction, is vital to the success of your vacation-home project.

5

Some locations, such as Lake Tahoe, offer year-round vacation opportunities.

Of course, no discussion of any building project is complete without an honest and thorough consideration of the financial implications. Chapter 3 presents the myriad costs of a vacation home, from purchasing land to caretaking, as well as calculating what you can afford and options for financing your dreams, if necessary.

From there, it's time to go on the road (or perhaps the Internet) and actually find a place to match your initial planning. Chapter 4 helps make the transition from your rough concept to reality as you investigate and narrow your choice of locations and follow through the process of finding and purchasing a particular homesite or parcel.

All of the planning stages, coupled with your chosen homesite, are essential to begin the process of designing your vacation home. Besides the traditional route of hiring an architect or building designer, Chapter 5 explores several alternatives to creating your blueprints, from house plan services to kit home manufacturers and computer software. Regardless, the result is a set of working drawings that will

The result of all your hard work is a finished home, one that hopefully remains true to your initial goals.

be used to secure permits and approvals, as well as negotiate the actual construction of your second home with a builder.

Advice abounds, from books and pamphlets to Internet chat rooms, about how to hire a contractor. With vacation homes, in particular, that process is as much about "how" to as it is "where" to, with regards to the pros and cons of hiring a builder in the location of your vacation home versus one operating closer to your primary residence. Chapters 5 and 6 not only offer a reasonable recipe for successfully hiring any contractor, but the latter chapter also outlines the people, paperwork and process that drive your vacation-home project.

Regardless of your experience in dealing with design and building professionals, the result of all your hard work is a finished home, one that hopefully remains true to your initial goals and ideals for a vacation retreat. But the work isn't over. While a second home should not require the kind of intensive care of a primary residence, there are warranty and long-term maintenance issues, as defined in Chapter 7, that you'll need to consider as you settle in and enjoy the fruits of your labor.

Modern design and materials have made it easier to marry form and function in vacation homes.

By the end of this book, you should have a clear picture of the entire process for conceiving, creating and maintaining your ideal vacation home—and whether you're up to the task. That's not meant to scare you off. Rather, this book is designed to be a realistic and honest approach to building a second home that satisfies your need to relax and, for at least a few days a month, get off the fast track and enjoy a slower pace. 🔆

A Home Away From Home

Photo by Brad Simmons Photography/Lok-N-Log Homes

A vacation home should free you from the pressures of your day-to-day life and allow you to relax in comfort and beauty.

There's a reason a single-family home is the most popular route people take to create a vacation getaway. Simply, a true second home satisfies particular and personal needs and desires, offering the utmost convenience and freedom. You can literally go there whenever you want. And when you get there, your stuff—not someone else's mass-market decorating scheme or threadbare, plaid-upholstered sofabed—is waiting for you. It's comfortable; it's yours.

The other difference between second homes and other vacation getaway options is proximity. Despite dreams (or delusions) of a thatch-roof hut on a far-off tropical island, most vacation homeowners stay fairly close to their primary residences—where, within a 200-mile radius, they usually find an ideal setting for a second home. Those looking to travel afar for vacation typically choose other housing options and use them less often and for longer stretches of time.

If your dream is to create a getaway for yourself, whether you're single, a couple or a family, it is important to remain focused on those goals and essentially block out (or at least make secondary) other considerations that threaten to muddy your concept and divide your loyalties toward achieving a true vacation retreat.

Primary Considerations

There are three primary considerations for building a vacation home that will allow you to get away from the routines and pressures of your everyday life. They cover issues of comfort and convenience, proximity for short-term relaxation, and ownership in something you created from your own imagination.

Consideration One

First, your vacation home needs to be a comfortable retreat that is accessible at any given time. Therefore, it must be close enough to your primary residence to allow a last-minute decision to jump in the car on a Friday afternoon and arrive at your second home in time for a late dinner. If that image is your ideal, make it your top priority and etch it in your brain as you delve deeper into the process. No doubt it will be challenged.

Consideration Two

To help strengthen that resolve, the second consideration regards why you want or need a vacation home. To relax, right? And probably not for a week or two, but more likely for long weekends throughout the year. As Americans, we are more productive and work harder and longer, with less allowable time off, than folks in other developed countries. We have a devotion to our work that can border on obsessive.

And in an increasingly fast-paced, downsizing, high-expectation working world, taking more than a few days off can make us feel uneasily detached from our jobs or careers—and might even be professionally risky. Simply, we typically don't need a whole week or more to decompress from work stress; taking a short drive into a rural setting, nestling in comfortable surroundings and puttering around for a few days usually does the trick.

Photo by Rich Binsacca

Spectacular natural settings, such as Idaho's Sawtooth Mountains (near Stanley, Idaho), provide a backdrop for many vacation home-owners.

To achieve that nirvana, however, means having it close by. A second-home sanctuary within three hours driving time affords ready access and requires little effort, not to mention the same currency. The drive itself may even serve as an emotional and logistical transition from work to relaxation.

And, with a retreat just a few hours away, long weekends serve to satisfy the need for relaxation without the pressure of lugging work with us on vacation in the form of laptops, Palm Pilots and cellular phones.

By contrast, rushing to the airport and renting a car, or even contemplating a drive of six hours or longer, makes

Long weekends serve to satisfy the need for relaxation.

it too easy to rationalize staying at home and trying to relax there, resisting the urge to check e-mail or go into the office "just for a few hours" on a weekend. Good luck.

A potential hitch in this scenario can be a perception that your ideal vacation home setting is somewhere far away, like the tropics or the south of France. It's remarkable what you can find in a relatively tight radius from your primary residence, and what's close enough to that

From the overall design to the color on the walls, your personal style should come through in your vacation home.

spot to hold your interest, provide entertainment, shopping and services and offer a variety of recreational opportunities.

Chances are if you live in a mountainous state, such as Colorado or Idaho, or in the Midwest or near the Great Lakes, you'll be attracted to what those areas offer in terms of second-home locations. Sure, an occasional visit to the ocean from an inland state can be an exciting change of pace. But human nature (and survey data) says if you build a second home there, you'll use it infrequently and worse, open a Pandora's box of worries and rationalizations that will detract from the primary goal of owning a second home.

Consideration Three

The third consideration on the vacation home priority list is equally critical: that you own it and, beyond that, have a hand in its design and development.

If you're in a financial position to have a vacation home, you're also likely in a position to create what you want. Building your own second home further differentiates this vacation option from a resort condo or timeshare, and even from an existing home built for someone else. (See "Building versus Buying," page 13)

Few things will add greater value to your vacation home than placing your personal stamp on the project. The work put into its development from start to finish will no doubt connect you to the house beyond having your name on the deed.

Few things will add greater value to your vacation home than placing your personal stamp on the project.

Building versus Buying

Is it better to build new, or buy an existing home to use as your vacation getaway? With available land becoming more scarce in some of the most desirable vacation areas, and more than six million vacation homes already built, looking at an existing home is tempting—assuming you can find one that meets your needs and, even more important, fulfill your dreams.

Any home built with the imprint of its owners includes features and other quirks endearing to them, but perhaps not to anyone else. Those elements are what make a vacation home special to its owners. For a new owner, such details sometimes can be swapped out or altered in a remodeling effort. Existing structural elements and floor plans, however, are more difficult (and expensive) to mold into your ideal second home.

In addition to cosmetic changes, an existing home also may need some mechanical upgrades to meet modern-day standards and lifestyle needs. Progress in the areas of heating and cooling equipment, fire protection, appliances and electrical and telecommunications services can boost a remodeling budget beyond the cost of building a new home.

The two key considerations in the buy-versus-build debate are location and cost. As you search for a location and homesite, weigh the value of an ideal parcel with the price tag of remodeling the existing house on the land you covet, remembering to add that cost to what you're already paying for the developed property.

The other side of that coin is having to compromise on a less attractive, if empty, parcel for the sake of building a new vacation home on that piece of ground. Certainly, the cost of a raw (if improved) parcel is less than that of an existing home, and building a house on that land can be as affordable as it needs to be (see Chapter 3 regarding costs and affordability).

Of course, the ability to move in right away to an existing home, even if it fails to measure up to your ideal, must be considered against the long-term commitment of designing and building your own vacation home. As you progress through this process, the right choice for you and your family will almost certainly present itself.

Without the limitations of a predetermined list of design options presented by a resort developer or the burden of designing and decorating a home for renters or resale, your vacation home can provide the comfortable setting and lifestyle requisite to achieving the relaxation you need (and want) in a home away from home.

Of course, it is entirely possible that you may find among the six-plus million existing second homes out there one that meets your every need, desire and expectation—and is still within a three-hour drive from home. As available land continues to get gobbled up, that option may someday be your only one. But not today.

Second-home lots, or parcels, may be getting more expensive in some places, but they aren't yet scarce enough in most locations to merit trading in your dreams for someone else's vision of an ideal vacation home. If you're considering a second-home purchase, you likely have the means to execute your own vision.

Challenges

As you work your way into the process of creating your vacation home, certain considerations will challenge your primary goals. The lure of potential market appreciation and high resale value, a lucrative second income from rentals, new and exciting recreational activities and even retirement fantasies will rear up to block your vision. While many of these considerations are valid, they ultimately undermine your ability to create a true vacation retreat for yourself and your family.

Challenge 1: Second Homes as Investment Property

In terms of resale, second homes historically are a bad bet, appreciating in value much less than your primary residence. True, there just so many ocean and lakefront lots to go around, and wilderness and other rural areas are primary targets for environmental and conservation efforts to limit growth and control development. But the outskirts will

Considering a second home's potential resale value handicaps the design-build process.

never be as desirable as developed urban and suburban areas. They may be wickedly expensive up front, but overall their value over time is likely to appreciate more slowly than a home located in a metropolitan area.

In fact, according to surveys by the American Resort Development Association, only about 18 percent of current and potential vacation homeowners envision their homes as investment property within the first few years of occupancy, and even less so in the longer term.

Custom Log Home
40 acres with view

Mike Gamblin Real Estate
378-9100

While many vacation homes are resold, the long-term appreciation of a second home is generally less than with a primary residence.

Overwhelmingly, they want it for their own recreation and vacation pleasure. So, when you build a vacation home, do it for your emotional and spiritual wellbeing. If financial benefits accrue, so much the better.

In addition, considering a second home's potential resale value handicaps the design-build process. Instead of serving just your needs, you and your design professional must also figure in some mass-market features that may be contrary to your particular lifestyle preferences.

Any home built with the imprint of its owners includes features and other quirks endearing to them, but perhaps not to anyone else.

For instance, you may only want or need two bedrooms, but a family with different needs may be looking for at least a three-bedroom home, or perhaps something smaller. Even common elements to a vacation home, such as stairs, lofts, wood-burning heat sources and floor coverings can impact its resale value. No one's tastes and needs are exactly the same; if they were, we'd all buy timeshares instead of preferring to build our own getaways.

15

Challenge 2: Rental Income Potential

Like unrealistic resale aspirations, banking on a boatload of rental income from a vacation home is, at best, deceptive. At worst, owning off-site rental property puts your home at risk from damage and excessive wear from unknown occupants, attaches extra tax burdens and other legal stipulations that sap some of that income, limits your ability to actually stay in your own vacation home, and adds the stress of assuming the role of a landlord. Essentially, offering your vacation home as a rental undermines the point of owning it in the first place. Just try to sleep well with some stranger's family in your second home.

The lure, of course, is money. Vacation home rentals are a big business in popular destinations, and homeowners can often cover their annual mortgage, property tax, insurance and maintenance costs in just one rental season.

The question to ask, then, is whether you want your vacation home to be a retreat or a business. If it's the latter, first talk to your tax advisor and learn about specific, yet complex, guidelines that the Internal Revenue Service uses to regulate income property, among other issues, including property management and lease agreements.

And, as with a home built for resale instead of relaxation, a secondary residence earmarked for income also needs to appeal to a broader audience than you and your family. In addition to making it accessible inside and out to a variety of potential occupants, you'll also want to outfit it with appliances, finishes and furnishings that can either take a lot of abuse or are nearly disposable. This could become a decorating scheme that is both bland and uncomfortable, and a far cry from how you would have the house if you were its sole (or primary) occupant.

In fact, so discouraging and limiting are the tax laws and other factors relating to rental property that the percentage of vacation home owners interested in that option has been decreased by half since 1990.

Challenge 3: Recreational Illusions

While it is important to find a vacation-home location that puts your favorite recreational activities close by (if not right outside your door), placing too high a priority on recreation can affect your choice of settings. Specifically, selecting an area primarily because it offers a wide variety of activities, such as in a resort development, may locate your vacation home too far away and limit your ability to get there for a quick weekend stay.

Besides, most of what you want to do (if anything, outside of a few long walks or perhaps a morning run) is probably going to be close by, any-

You may think you'll tackle a new recreational activity on vacation, but chances are you'll stick with what you're most comfortable doing on vacation.

way. I'm reminded of a vacation cabin in a planned development of second homes near Donner Lake, just below Lake Tahoe in California. It is accessible to a half-dozen golf courses, a few public tennis courts, some of the world's best winter and summer recreational activities, and even the gaming industry just over the border in Nevada—all within an hour's drive, and often less.

The last time I stayed at that cabin, the second home of a family friend, my "activities" consisted of one round of (bad) golf and relaxing with a book on Donner's tiny lakefront beach. The point is, I still did what I wanted instead of trying to participate in all that the area has to offer. On vacation, especially one as accessible as a nearby second home, filling your schedule with activities often runs counter to relaxation.

It may be tempting to envision yourself wind-surfing on a mountain lake, or kayaking the ocean waves or a series of river rapids or taking up golf or tennis simply because such facilities are part of a vacation-home development. But for most of us creatures of habit, such visions will remain just

Filling your schedule with activities often runs counter to relaxation.

A vacation home can accommodate families, but beware of building something too large for the majority of your stays.

that, and what we prefer to do on vacation is likely to be found within a reasonable proximity.

Challenge 4: A Family Retreat

As with other challenges to your top vacation home priorities and goals, bowing to the temptation to create a family compound instead of an intimate, quiet second-home retreat will, of course, alter your course. Designing a home to acommodate everyone at one time will expand your home and its budget, as well as muddy your personal vision for the home's layout and look.

Historically and statistically, however, most folks avoid this snare; the vast majority of vacation homes (more than three-quarters, in fact) are built or planned with two bedrooms or less, with the trend actually moving toward one-bedroom and studio-sized units. In part, such numbers can be attributed to the maturity of most second-home owners, who typically are 40 and older.

That said, a vacation home can be a family retreat, just not one designed to accommodate everyone at one time. As non-income property, your second home can be used by family and friends, without any IRS or other restrictions, when you're not there—providing you with an opportunity to invite close friends to enjoy a quiet weekend getaway, or allowing your older children a vacation alternative.

If you are inclined to expand the accommodations, consider sleeping lofts and porches instead of formal bedrooms, which can serve as storage or sitting areas when the masses depart. Even furnishings, such as sleeper-sofas and futons in the living (or "public") areas of the house, can provide adequate sleeping arrangements without the permanency of placing beds in additional private rooms.

Photo by Northeastern Log Homes

The beauty of a vacation home is not only its setting, but also what it allows you to enjoy.

Challenge 5:
Retirement

It seems logical: with your vacation home nearby, in a more relaxed and often recreational setting, built to smaller scale but still outfitted with some comforts of home, you may consider it the ideal place to retire. In fact, nearly half of vacation homeowners foresee such a progression.

Whatever your passion, whether it be fishing or shopping, look for an area that offers that and other recreational activities you like.

In some cases, that scenario plays out fine. The age-restricted housing developments that dot the desert Southwest, for instance, are often sold to folks in their fifties as seasonal or vacation homes (if often far away from their primary residences) with an eye toward a permanent move in retirement. But for the rest of us, adding the burden of accommodating a retirement lifestyle in your vacation home plans can impact its location and design.

From a location perspective, a rural or otherwise remote area might seem optimum for a weekend getaway, but often lacks sophisticated medical and other services that might be needed once you occupy the house after retirement and beyond. Considering the availability of those services, as well as convenient and swift access by family and friends in times of extra-care needs (such as a temporary disability) will limit your choices of potential vacation home locations and home sites.

Also, the house itself might be hard to get to and get into, with a steep driveway or a walk-up entry that is easily navigated as an active adult, but which becomes a barrier or hazard later in life. Inside, similar accessibility issues come into play. If you envision eventually retiring in your vacation home, its interior design and layout will need to accommodate those plans. The result is a compromise of your current needs, desires and abilities to oblige those in an uncertain, if anticipated, future. Chances are, neither lifestyle will be properly or completely served.

Building Your Dream

If anything, a commitment to the three core considerations of a vacation home retreat—that it be a place for relaxation and respite, located within a few hundred miles of your primary residence and carry your personal stamp—all but mandates that you design and build it from the ground up.

While you may be able to find an existing home that also meets that criteria (or can be remodeled, if the location is too good to pass up), you're certain to get what you want if you start fresh and with your own vision of an ideal second home (see "Building versus Buying," page 13).

That kind of undertaking, however, requires commitment. Financial demands aside, building a vacation home takes an emotional and even physical toll. Unlike buying a pre-designed or already-built home in a resort subdivision, much less a timeshare condo, the process requires active participation every step of the way. There are land purchase and use negotiations, meetings with design professionals

The process requires active participation every step of the way.

and contractors and umpteen trips to the building site to evaluate the home's construction progress. It may take a year or more to get it designed and built.

Preparation for this marathon begins with a thorough and honest evaluation of what you need and want from a vacation home—and whether it is even an appropriate option at all.

A LIFESTYLE PROFILE

Courtesy Northeastern Log Homes

Achieving your ideal second home begins with determining and prioritizing your vacation lifestyle preferences and needs.

Creating a Lifestyle Profile is a key step toward determining the location and creating the actual design of your vacation home. The process also provides an opportunity to make an honest assessment of whether a second home is really the best option for you and your family.

By taking time to document your past vacation experiences and recognizing patterns that emerge from those memories, you'll be better able to narrow and prioritize what you want and need in a vacation home. With that information, you can begin to visualize an ideal setting and build a file of ideas, notes, articles, house plans and other images that support that vision.

Vacation Memories

If I try hard enough, I can place myself on the cushions of the wraparound bench in the living room of that house at Sea Ranch (some

Some of your fondest vacation memories, such as a spectacular lake view, can often be translated into the context of a vacation-home location and design.

years after my driving epiphany), with my three-year-old son intently watching my brother pluck away at a guitar. When I drive into the Sierras, I am reminded of the homes we rented there, including one in which I recuperated from a rafting accident. I also remember family car trips up into the glaciers of Canada and into the depths of the Canyonlands of the Southwestern U.S., and, most recently, taking my kids to Disneyland for the first time.

No doubt you have similar memories, perhaps not always in the context of a vacation home and maybe not always pleasant. You may recall journeying to a theme park one summer, visiting faraway relatives, exploring dramatic natural wonders or a host of other activities and travels. Now, it's time to conjure up those memories, from as far back and in as much detail as you can remember.

Make a List
The process is as simple as getting legal pad and pen, or perhaps settling in at your computer, and making a list. It requires no particular rhyme or reason, though chronologically is often an easy route to help release some far-gone vacation memories (see Vacation Memories form and sample, pages 25 and 27).

Conjure up memories, from as far back and in as much detail as you can remember.

And, while it may be somewhat unpleasant, also jot down those experiences that, for one reason or another, you'd just as soon forget—and certainly want to avoid repeating (see "The Value of Bad Vacations," page 28).

Vacation Memories

Use this form or create your own; make multiple copies to capture as many vacation memories as possible (good and bad), dating back as far as you wish. Use the Notes section to jot down any special circumstances or occurrences.

Date _____ Overall Grade: _____

Place _____ Time of Year _____

Transportation _____ Travel time _____

Lodging _____ How long? _____

Activities _____

Who went? _____

Meals _____

Notes:

Date _____ Overall Grade: _____

Place _____ Time of Year _____

Transportation _____ Travel time _____

Lodging _____ How long? _____

Activities _____

Who went? _____

Meals _____

Notes:

Date _____ Overall Grade: _____

Place _____ Time of Year _____

Transportation _____ Travel time _____

Lodging _____ How long? _____

Activities _____

Who went? _____

Meals _____

Notes:

Recalling good (and bad) vacation memories takes time, as some of the most valuable experiences may have occurred long ago, even in childhood.

As you create your list of past vacations, try to include as much detail as possible: how you got there (e.g., by car, plane or other mode); the time of year; where you stayed and for how long; what you did on that vacation, from recreational sports to sightseeing and shopping; and who went with you, whether it be family members, your sister's latest boyfriend or a group of buddies. Any other details—how long it took to get there, any hassles or hurdles along the way, what you ate and whether you cooked or went out—also are helpful. Leave some space for notes to add in any extra circumstances about each vacation.

> *Allow yourself time to let the memories come to you rather than forcing all of them out at once.*

Making this list might take awhile, and you should allow yourself time to let the memories come to you rather than forcing all of them out at once. Carry a small notepad or even a microcassette tape recorder to capture them (or at least their inkling) during less-than-convenient moments. Use photographs and other memorabilia to help jar loose your memory. With that, dedicate some time each day, perhaps just 15 minutes, to jot down or type in your vacation memories. Chances are, you'll remember more than you thought possible.

While most of your memories will likely be of dramatic, long-term vacations (a trip to Hawaii or Mexico, an Alaskan cruise, perhaps a tour of Europe or the Orient), also make note of long weekends you stayed at the cabin of a family friend or rented because it was near some great snow skiing, water sports or natural scenery. And account for any spontaneous jaunts to a nearby resort town or other getaway destination, if

Vacation Memories

Date	August 2000	Overall Grade:	B-
Place	Richardson Res.	Time of Year	summer
Transportation	Rental Car/plane (Reno)	Travel time	1 hr plane, 1 hr drive
Lodging	Tent	How long?	4 days
Activities	Swimming, hiking, campfires, waterskiing		
Who went?	Whole family (10 total)		
Meals	Camp meals		
Notes:	Very dirty; took cool tour of old gold mine; stayed at C & J's cabin on last night		

Date	September 2000	Overall Grade:	A-
Place	McCall, ID	Time of Year	late summer
Transportation	Car	Travel time	2 hrs (one-way)
Lodging	D&J's House	How long?	overnight
Activities	Went out to dinner; videos @ home, walked town		
Who went?	me & K; D&J with Melissa (5 total)		
Meals	out; breakfast next day (cooked)		
Notes:	Very relaxing, very nice drive — great just to get away.		

Date	June '99	Overall Grade:	B+
Place	Disneyland	Time of Year	summer
Transportation	plane to LA	Travel time	90 mins (one-way)
Lodging	Disneyland Hotel	How long?	3 + days
Activities	Disneyland, swam in pool		
Who went?	me & kids, Mom & Dad (5 total)		
Meals	mostly @ hotel & park		
Notes:	A good place for kids, took monorail & tram to park, coffee w/Dad in the mornings. Hotel very nice.		

just overnight. In fact, those instances might be among your fondest memories—and also bode well if you're considering a vacation home.

Identifying Patterns

Once you're satisfied with your list, create a system for ranking or prioritizing each vacation experience. A simple scale from 1-10 or an academic-like A-F grading scheme both work well. Try to judge each memory on its own merit rather than in comparison to others on the list; if you end up with a lot of As (or 1s), so be it. Ranking or rating your various vacation memories will start the process of identifying your patterns and preferences, leading you toward a profile that is either compatible with or runs counter to a vacation-home lifestyle.

If you like, also rank or rate the particular elements, or categories, of each vacation. For instance, you may have enjoyed the vacation spot once you got there, but the travel involved was stressful, long or uncomfortable—or vice versa. Maybe you stayed too long, or not long enough.

Once you complete your rankings, group all of the "A" or top-rated vacations (or particular elements of them) and look for similarities. In particular, make note of general commonalities regarding how far and how long in travel time, as well as accommodations and recreational or other activities. To make that process easier, record them under a few broad categories, such as Destination or Travel, as well as House versus Hotel and By Car as opposed to other modes of transportation, and so on—whatever describes them best in your case.

The Value of Bad Vacations

We've all experienced them, those vacations that simply didn't work out. Where every step was a struggle and stress, and we ended up more tired than when we left home. But there's value in those experiences, and they should be included and assessed along with your "A" list vacations to identify elements to avoid—a little reminder about what you don't like.

More so than vacations that were wholly horrible, you'll probably find that certain elements ruined those trips, such as language barriers, lack of activities, weather or perhaps too long a stay. As an extra little exercise, follow the same process with these experiences as you are with your fondest vacation memories to further complete your Lifestyle Profile.

How long you stayed also is important, though don't be surprised if you find most of your past vacations have been a week or longer. Without the benefit of a second home within a few hours from a primary residence, most of us tend to stay away longer and travel farther, if less frequently, on vacation.

Vacation Memories

Date   August 2000   Overall Grade: B-

Place   Richardson Res.   Time of Year   summer

Transportation Rental Car/plane (Reno) Travel time   1 hr plane, 1 hr drive

Lodging   Tent   How long?   4 days

Activities   Swimming, hiking, campfires, waterskiing

Who went?   Whole family (10 total)

Meals   Camp meals

Notes: Very dirty; took cool tour of old gold mine, stayed at C & J's cabin
                on last night

Date   September 2000   Overall Grade: A-

Place   McCall, ID   Time of Year   late summer

Transportation Car   Travel time   2 hrs (one-way)

Lodging   D&J's House   How long?   overnight

Activities   Went out to dinner; videos @ home, walked town

Who went?   me & K; D&J with Melissa (5 total)

Meals   out; breakfast next day (cooked)

Notes: Very relaxing, very nice drive — great just to get away.

Date   June '99   Overall Grade: B+

Place   Disneyland   Time of Year   summer

Transportation plane to LA   Travel time   90 mins (one-way)

Lodging   Disneyland Hotel   How long?   3 + days

Activities   Disneyland, swam in pool

Who went?   me & kids, Mom & Dad (5 total)

Meals   mostly @ hotel & park

Notes: A good place for kids, took monorail & tram to park, coffee w/Dad
                in the mornings. Hotel very nice.

29

Similarly, it may surprise you to find out that, while vacations often hold the promise of allowing us to do whatever we want, most of us tend to enjoy the same activities over and over, indicating what we really like to do instead of what we might fantasize about or envision doing on vacation. That said, past activities such as golf or tennis, fishing and other water sports, skiing or snowmobiling all are good indicators that a vacation home might be for you.

If anything, this somewhat formal process allows you to remain objective and honest about emerging patterns and truly assess whether to invest more in the process of creating a vacation home or simply stop right here (see "Walking Away," below).

Even so, our lifestyles can change. As a younger person, couple or family, you may have taken vacations that fit a past lifestyle, to entertain the kids or see the world. Therefore, make note of how long it's been since you took those vacations, as well as those taken more recently. By now, perhaps, you've settled down and are looking for relaxation rather than excitement or long travel. Still, if you haven't yet acted on that lifestyle change—if you still prefer and take overseas vacations as opposed to weekend getaways to nearby resort towns—this process will expose those tendencies.

Walking Away

The process of ranking your past vacation memories and tracking emerging preferences or tendencies may, in fact, lead you away from the idea of creating a vacation retreat. If you begin to see that, for the most part, you enjoy vacations that take you far from home and include a hotel stay and sightseeing, perhaps investing in a vacation home a few hours from your primary residence is out of line with your true preferences.

Trust the process by being honest in your assessment of your vacation memories, and resist temptations to manipulate your findings and patterns to suit what you think you want rather than what appears to be your ideal or preferred vacation experiences. If you find that a second home isn't for you, be willing to walk away from that path. You can always come back to it later should your lifestyle needs and desires change.

Identifying Your Profile

With your "A" list comparison complete, you can create a basic Lifestyle Profile. In fact, it may already be apparent from your research, but actually documenting the elements of your vacation preferences will be a helpful template during the design phase of the process.

Keep it simple. Use your vacation categories to come up with a short, general statement that matches your tendencies. For instance, you may find that you most often like traveling in the summer, within your state or region, and for about a *Documenting your vacation preferences will be a helpful template during the design phase of the process.*
week at a time. You typically camp in a tent or rent a small tent-trailer, and hike, fish and swim on those vacations. Or, maybe you prefer to stay at a nearby resort condo and, in addition to those activities, take advantage of tennis or golf facilities or shopping.

(If you're game, create an "anti-" Lifestyle Profile out of your worst-case vacation elements and experiences, if only to crystallize those things you want to make sure to avoid in your planning.)

Recreational activities play an important role in determining your Lifestyle Profile and, in turn, the eventual location and design of your vacation home.

Study your own home (and others), especially key rooms like the kitchen, to determine your wants and needs in your vacation home.

Courtesy Northeastern Log Homes

With those generalities, also note some common exceptions that you feel add to your Lifestyle Profile, specifically recreational activities that you enjoy and have done on some of your vacations. And, of course, keep all of your notes. They may come in handy as you delve into the design and construction phases of your second-home project.

Wants and Needs

With your Lifestyle Profile complete, you can move on to the next planning stage—brainstorming a list of wants and needs. This assessment, along with your Profile, will give you and your design professional a clearer path toward creating your ideal retreat, as well as helping you imagine and eventually find an appropriate setting or location for your second home.

As you did in creating your Lifestyle Profile, allow some time to assess your wants and needs. Though some folks can brainstorm a near-complete list in one sitting, chances are you'll want that list to evolve over a few weeks or longer. Look for things you like (and don't like) as you visit other people's homes, take short drives into the country, talk to folks who own second homes and consider the kind of life you want in a vacation retreat. Your wants and needs assessment will subsequently fill out.

Allow your mind to wander and wish out loud; there's always time to rein yourself back.

One way to help spur the process is to categorize your wants and needs into three general areas: the home and its amenities and features; activities and recreation; and the culture, atmosphere and services of your ideal setting or location. That said, allow your mind to wander and wish out loud; there's always time to rein you back, if necessary, but no better opportunity to shoot for the moon.

The Home

The best way to start developing a Wants and Needs List about your second home is to take a look around your primary residence, as well as other homes you like (vacation or otherwise). With an eye toward what

Wants and Needs

Home

Pool table

Big windows (lake view)

Mud room (off garage; ski trips)

Covered porch

Breakfast nook (no dining room)

Hot tub/spa (on deck)

Barbecue grill

Spanish tile (kitchen floor, from Keri's house)

Maple cabinets

Outdoor shower

Berber carpet

Fireplace (2)

Wants and Needs: Home
Keep a separate list for those ideas, preferences and desires specific to your vacation home. Consider what you'll need in terms of bedrooms and sleeping areas, kitchen appliances, relaxation or activities and other amenities or features.

Your list of vacation "activities" can (and probably should) include relaxation and the simple enjoyment of your second home.

Courtesy Precision Craft Log Structures

you like to do or envision yourself doing on vacation in a home setting, start with the basics: the size and features of the kitchen; the number of bedrooms and why (or, even more abstractly, how many people will sleep there at a time, regardless of where); the number of common and private bathrooms. Also, ponder living (or "public") spaces, and whether there's a need for a formal dining room or a desire for a little niche or separate space for a library or memorabilia.

Better than anyone, you know what you like to do, especially on vacation.

To be sure, your list will be unique to you, and there are no rules at this point about the length, content or detail of your wants and needs assessment. You may already have an image of your vacation home etched in your mind, or maybe it's just a jumble of images and elements so far. You may list elements such as exposed beams, Spanish tile floors, a sleeping loft and a big fireplace without really knowing how (or if) those feature really fit together. That work comes later.

More than any other assessment, the one relating to your actual vacation home can and will evolve as you continue on with this process. You'll see something in a magazine or when visiting the home of friends or family that will further enhance your vision; even the smallest detail is appropriate. As with your Lifestyle Profile, carry a notepad or cassette recorder with you to help document those details and ideas, then add them to the master list.

Activities

Better than anyone, you know what you like to do, especially on vacation. Your Lifestyle Profile already has done some of the legwork here, and you also should remain mindful of those recreational opportunities that appear exciting but, in fact, you'll never actually do.

Again, however, this is a chance to brain-dump. If I was to quickly list those activities I most enjoy on vacation, it would include sleeping late, reading, occasionally playing some tennis or golf, biking and hiking, watching movies, cooking and enjoying the sunset from a comfortable chair on a deck or balcony without distraction or the pressures of time. Not a long list, to be sure, but an honest one, and there's probably more

Wants and Needs
Activities
Reading
Videos
Internet
Golf
Tennis
Fly fishing
Hiking/backpacking
Barbecue
Board games
Antiquing/browsing

Wants and Needs:
Activities
Keep a separate list for those recreational or other activities in which you envision participating while at your vacation home.

Often, the setting and the activities you most want and need go hand-in-hand.

I'm missing. Of course, your list will be different and specific to your favorite activities.

The key here is to list those things you want to do on vacation, as opposed to those activities you are compelled to do at your primary residence (such as yardwork and general maintenance, office work, bills and taxes, etc.). No doubt, most of those chores will be a part of owning a vacation home, but considering them now is unnecessary. This is a wish list.

Also, list separately those things you envision doing alone, as a couple and as a family or joined by friends. Together with your other Wants and Needs Lists, this assessment will not only help crystallize an ideal location for your second home, but help you and your design professional create a home environment that meets your expectations while satisfying a broader range of circumstances.

The area surrounding your eventual second home also is vital to its value as a retreat.

The Setting

Chances are you've given less thought to the setting or general location of your second home than to the home itself and your vacation activities. But the area surrounding your eventual second home also is vital to its value as a retreat.

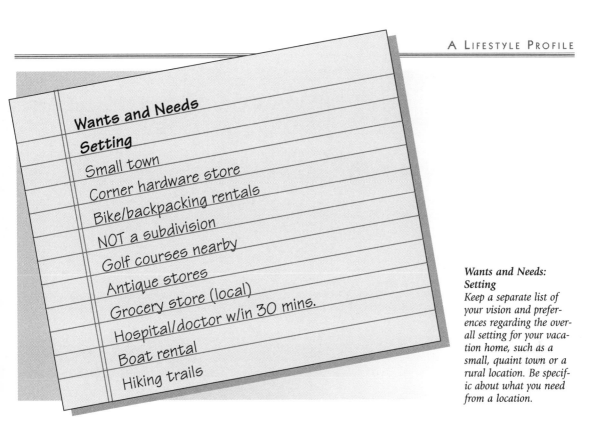

Wants and Needs

Setting

Small town

Corner hardware store

Bike/backpacking rentals

NOT a subdivision

Golf courses nearby

Antique stores

Grocery store (local)

Hospital/doctor w/in 30 mins.

Boat rental

Hiking trails

Wants and Needs: Setting
Keep a separate list of your vision and preferences regarding the overall setting for your vacation home, such as a small, quaint town or a rural location. Be specific about what you need from a location.

In a way, this particular assessment extends the Activities List by considering the services you want and need to have available to fulfill your vacation-home experience. It also considers issues of culture and atmosphere, access and privacy and other conveniences.

For instance, some folks envision a remote area, with few houses (much less a full-service town) nearby, to which they pack in whatever they need for their stay. Others like the idea of a small-town culture and having modern conveniences and shopping within a bike ride or short drive, or perhaps even walking distance, from their second home.

Again, allow your mind to unload, even if some wants and needs appear to conflict. For example, you may envision a very private and remote getaway tucked in the mountains or along a lake or river, but still have a desire or need to shop for groceries while you're there. Or, you may envision wandering the antique shops or dining at the folksy eateries of a small town, but want to avoid areas with mega-stores or video rental chains. (In my case, I don't need to eat out when I'm staying at a vacation home, but I'd like access to a daily newspaper.)

Setting
Small town
Bike rentals
NOT a subdivision
Grocery store (local)
Hiking trails

Activies
Reading
Videos
Tennis
Hiking/
Backpacking

Home
Pool table
Big windows (lake view)
Mud room (off garage;
ski trips)
Covered porch
Breakfast nook
(no dining room)
Maple cabinets
Fireplace (2)

Wants and Needs:
Priorities
Once you prioritize the
items on each of your
Wants and Needs Lists,
list the top ones together
on a single sheet.

An important consideration is the presence or proximity of emergency and medical services. Whether you're in your 30s or nearing your 60s, accidents and other crises can happen, even when you're not there (such as a fire). If you're considering your second home as a potential retirement home, access to such services—including doctors and hospitals—may be an even higher priority with regards to your home's location.

For the most part, however, this wish list of your ideal second-home setting should focus on the experience you envision there. While practical issues have their place, they should not overwhelm your ideal.

Prioritizing
As with the memories of past vacations, prioritize the items on your three wish lists, which will help you make choices later on when you actually consider and visit potential locations and homesites and begin the design-build process. Of course, your priorities may change as time goes on, but at least you'll have a solid baseline for evaluation when key decisions come up.

In addition, use your lists as guides to creating a Clip File to help put a visual reference to your wants and needs. Magazine or personal photos, postcards, house plan books, catalogs, maps and brochures, book-marked web sites and other memorabilia can be stored for the design process. Whatever you collect is appropriate, from cabinet knobs to clothing and furniture, as well as photos or other references to home styles, kitchen layouts and ideal views or settings. As with your other lists, allow your Clip File to evolve and grow over time.

Consider keeping your clip files separate to your three Wants and Needs Lists, though at some point a design professional (or you) will evaluate them together.

The Value

Creating a Lifestyle Profile, your Wants and Needs Lists, and a Clip File is essential to establishing your priorities for your second home. Some tough decisions and necessary trade-offs are on the horizon, and it will help to have some reminders to maintain your focus.

And while creating these lists and files might seem cumbersome and take longer than you want, it will pay off. Besides, there's plenty of work that can be done simultaneously, chiefly getting your financial house in order, establishing a realistic budget and securing financing for your vacation home.

REALITY CHECK: THE COSTS

Calculating your afford-ability, among other fiscal considerations, is necessary for determining the budget and financial needs for a vacation home.

To this point, you've been dreaming freely about your ideal vacation home. Now it's time to wake up to a dose of reality—the related costs and other financial considerations of building and owning a second home.

Just as proper planning streamlines the design and construction of your second home, adequate financial preparation will help you anticipate costs and tax obligations, and accurately calculate what you can afford. This chapter provides the entire financial picture, including several options within each step along the way. In the end, you'll be able to marry your dreams to your budget.

Primary versus Second Homes

Chances are you're already in a financial position that affords you to think about the possibility of owning a second home, if not the precise fiscal details involved. Though certainly, buying your primary residence gave you some insight into the process of purchasing a home and perhaps even that of having a house built for you.

In short, you're educated, financially secure and possess some experience with mortgage loans, insurance and perhaps even the home-building process—a stable base for the intricacies and quirks of a vacation-home project.

In contrast to your primary residence, however, second homes are viewed differently by landowners and developers, builders and contractors, utilities and municipal agencies, the IRS, insurance companies and lenders. That's primarily because vacation homes are considered a luxury for only occasional or seasonal use, and are thus a higher risk for everyone involved (including you) in terms of protecting that investment in property. Other factors, such as income from renting a second home, also impact cost considerations of a vacation-home project.

Up-front and Ongoing Costs

From purchasing a raw piece of land to calculating the value of your time to participate in the process of the design, construction and maintenance of a second home, there are several up-front and ongoing costs to consider. All of these must be balanced against the value of owning and enjoying a vacation home.

Up-front Costs

Land. More than likely, your homesite will be a parcel of developed or raw land being sold by a private landowner.

There are several up-front and on-going costs to consider. All of these must be balanced against the value of owning and enjoying a vacation home.

Developed land simply means that the parcel is ready or near-ready to build upon—perhaps even approved as such by a city or county authority—with the basic utility connections already brought to the location and included in the price of the parcel. (By general definition, "developed" land is different than "improved" land, which has services, as well as one or more built structures and other permanent features on the property.)

Raw land, by contrast, is undeveloped, which means that perhaps it must be cleared and leveled for a building pad and usually needs access

Photo by Rich Binsacca

Developing a homesite, including the installation of roads and utilities, is an important upfront cost you may have to incur.

(a road), utilities and other public or private services brought to it before construction of your second home can begin.

Occasionally, and especially in popular vacation or resort areas, subdivisions of developed homesites for second homes are available. However, such communities often impose rules regarding the overall size and design aesthetic of the homes being built there.

The price of land depends on a parcel's size (or acreage), features, access, development features and, of course, location (for more details on selecting a homesite, see Chapter 4). Regardless of how you purchase it—whether by cash, with a conventional or private loan, through a second or refinanced mortgage—you'll have to prove full ownership before you can develop the land further, begin construction and make other improvements. Financing options are explained later in this chapter.

Development and Services. In addition to the cost of the land, you may have to pay to gain access to municipal utilities and other services, or develop them privately, such as a well and/or septic system. Unless you're planning to build in a very remote area, chances are you can tap the local electric, water, sewer and phone services. It may be that these and other utilities are already "stubbed up" at the edge of your property line, waiting to be connected to your home.

Photo by Rich Binsacca

Even in rural locations and scattered homesites, be sure to check out all of the land-use regulations and proximity to available utilities in your land purchase calculation.

However, if you are outside the service area or grid of such utilities, you'll need to either provide them or, in some cases, do without. Water and sewer (or septic) services are probably the first necessities, so careful planning and cost considerations for digging a well and developing a dedicated waste-disposal and treatment system is in order. (In fact, an excellent resource is the book, *Building Your Country Home*, which goes into complete technical detail about wells and septic systems. See the Bibliography on page 178 for more information.)

First, you'll want a documented report on the location and depth of the water table for the well, and will probably want to find a local contractor to do the job. If wells are the norm in the area, there are likely a few local folks around to dig them. Similarly, a septic system supplier and installer also will be nearby. Ask the seller and neighbors who have such systems, and also consult the phone book or a local real estate office to find reputable contractors and suppliers.

Of the other utilities, electricity is often the next priority. Some popular or established wilderness areas, as well as ocean or lakeside towns, have power lines strung up to serve residents and businesses, so tapping in is only a matter of paying the local utility to bring it to your property.

More remote or less-populated areas, however, are often outside the power grid. Drawing electricity from the nearest power source can be expensive and time-consuming. You may have to wait until there's enough development like yours to merit extending the lines to serve it.

If electricity is problematic because of cost and installation issues, perhaps a dedicated home generator or propane tank, supplied and installed locally, can serve your needs for lighting, cooking and water heating. Increasingly, solar or photovoltaic systems can reasonably serve the same purposes (albeit for low power-using appliances) or supplement a local utility or primary private system to reduce costs, especially ongoing utility expenses (see "The New Solar," below).

The New Solar

Forget that image of an aluminum-encased solar panel extending intrusively from a rooftop as an alternative way to deliver electricity. As vacation homes become more popular, even wilderness and remote areas will frown on such aesthetic faux pas, regardless of their energy benefits. Still, in some areas, tapping the sun's energy may be the best, or perhaps the only, way to bring power to your second home.

Today's new solar and photovoltaic (PV) systems for the home are, in fact, much less intrusive and better targeted to specific electrical functions and needs. While a PV system may never make economic sense as a whole-house energy source (the payback on such systems is at least the length of your mortgage loan), it can be used as back-up or for intermittent power, to run small appliances such as attic fans and security lighting or even to lower your electric bill.

The latest solar roof panels can now be designed to nearly match the profiles and dimensions of metal and asphalt composite shingle roofing materials. And, they install flush to those finishes (no shiny aluminum frames). Such panels (or sections of solar cells) can collect and store electricity in batteries, which can be used to power the lights only at night, leaving daylight as the lighting source when the sun's up. One company has even developed a pleasant-looking sunroom with a subtle pattern of solar cells, which can either power the water heater or supplement the power grid. In almost all instances, the payback on investment in today's newest solar and PV systems is much shorter than for yesterday's whole-house models.

Of course, you may want to enjoy your second-home getaway without the convenience (and cost) of electricity or any power source, preferring only daylight and maybe a few candles at night, a simple wood stove for space heating and cooking, and cold (or no) showers. It might be difficult to fathom, but you can, in fact, do without electricity or other power in your vacation-home retreat.

You can, in fact, do without electricity or other power in your vacation-home retreat.

Other "essential" services can, without a doubt, be done without. If you're attracted to an area remote enough to need private water, septic and propane power services, do you really need (or even want) telephone, data and cable television services or even a satellite dish? If your goal is to get away from it all, eliminating those services will not only enhance that lifestyle choice but also eliminate the cost to install and maintain them. Among those, only a telephone is perhaps a logical priority, as it is useful in reporting emergencies and can double as a fax and Internet line if needed or desired.

Of course, popular vacation and resort areas are hip to your "needs," and have taken steps to provide non-essential services and utilities to those who want and can afford them. Ever-improving satellite and wireless or fiber-optic telecommunications technology is widening the net of access to an almost universal scale, allowing small towns and remote areas to tap into the latest sources for information and entertainment.

Wrangling all these utilities and services on your own can be a burden. Costs are relative to your homesite, its proximity to the services you want and need and the time it takes to install them. If you are considering a raw parcel in a remote location, however, you may be able to negotiate with the seller (or landowner) to provide full or basic utility services as a condition of purchasing the land—with the price of the parcel appropriately adjusted to cover such costs—relieving you of the burden of finding and paying for their installation piecemeal or over time.

Fees and Taxes. Other costs for purchasing land and eventually building and owning a second home are the myriad fees and taxes assessed on your property. Of course, once you own the land (and perhaps even as you pay off a private loan to a landowner), you'll be responsible for property taxes on that parcel depending on its value. Most fees are one-time costs, while taxes (such as insurance) are ongoing expenses.

A homesite in a remote or wilderness area will likely have less of a property tax burden than an oceanfront or lakeside lot, but generally taxes on raw and unimproved land are much less than those with homes or buildings on the property regardless of location. Once you build your second home, of course, the value of the property will increase—and so will your tax bill. By that time, however, your annual property taxes will most likely be paid through your mortgage payment.

Other fees may creep up, as well. Some communities charge a one-time "impact" fee to pay for the extension of infrastructure (roads, shared utilities and other common services) to your site. However, impact fees

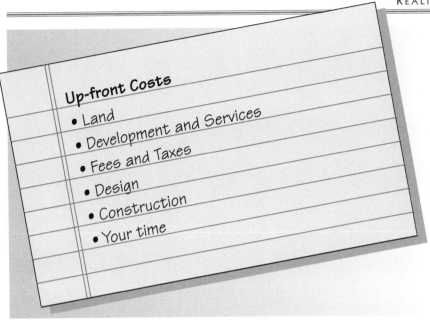

Up-front Costs
- Land
- Development and Services
- Fees and Taxes
- Design
- Construction
- Your time

For the most part, up-front costs are one-time expenses, some of which (like construction) often require outside financing and, in the case of your time, non-monetary sacrifices.

are most often charged to developers of multi-lot subdivisions, not individual landowners—though the cost may be passed along to you, the buyer, in the price of the parcel.

In addition, there will likely be costs for architectural review and plan approval (also called a code check), obtaining building permits and perhaps inspections during construction. If you purchase land in a planned-unit resort development, make sure to budget for annual association or community dues or fees, as well.

When considering your overall financial calculations, be aware of all local, county and state-imposed fees.

The bottom line: when considering your overall financial calculations for a second home, be aware of all local, county and state-imposed fees or other taxes that are your responsibility as a land and eventual property owner.

Of course, many fees and taxes are deductible from your personal income tax, though such deductions may be affected by how you use your vacation home, such as for investment property (as a rental) or simply personal use (see "What the IRS Says," page 62).

Design. Regardless of how you secure the blueprints or construction documents for your second home, there will be a cost attached. Simpler methods, such as stock house plans and kit homes, are much less expensive than using the services of a professional, licensed residential

Photo by Town & Country Cedar Homes

Whichever option you choose for the design and construction phases of your project, be prepared and willing to discuss your budget and other financial issues up front.

architect. His or her fee may be upwards of 20 percent of the total project budget. Chapter 5 goes into greater detail about the variety of options for generating plans for your vacation home, as well as the relative costs associated with each.

In some cases—especially on homesites that border the water, are on a severe slope or sit near a fault line—the design phase also will require the services (and costs) of a structural engineer. Such services, or at least an engineer's review and "stamp" of approval on the final building plans, may be stipulated by local code or building ordinances to ensure adequate structural support and construction of your second home under extreme, unusual or potentially hazardous conditions (such as an earthquake or flood).

Construction. As with design services, there are several options for building your home, each with a different cost. While Chapter 6 details those choices, suffice it to say that acting as your own contractor is not the cheapest way to go; in fact, it may actually be more expensive, and is certainly more time-consuming, than hiring a reputable builder or construction manager.

Even if you have considerable interest and skill in carpentry or building, ask yourself if it's really worth your free time—away from family, friends and activities—to manage the day-to-day responsibilities of your vacation-home project.

Construction is often the most expensive part of the entire process—and usually takes the most amount of time to complete, as well.

No matter what method you choose, the basic costs for constructing a home consist of management and coordination of the project, materials and equipment, labor, changes (called change orders or special orders), waste and debris removal and the builder's profit and operating costs. For a vacation home in a remote area, or even in a more popular destination, there also may be costs for transportation and related expenses for both labor and materials, temporary power and other services and heavy equipment for clearing the lot, if necessary. Once you select a building method, the precise costs for construction will be made clearer.

Courtesy Trus Joist

Ongoing Costs
Unless you pay in full with cash for your vacation home, its biggest ongoing expense is likely going to be the mortgage

payment. Just like the mortgage payment on your primary residence, it will include interest, insurance and taxes in addition to the loan premium (see "Financing" for more details, page 63). Beyond that, however, there are other ongoing costs to consider.

Maintenance and Upkeep. The completion of a second home signals the end of certain, one-time costs and activities (such as design and construction) and the beginning of new, ongoing expenses. As with your primary residence, there will be year-round utility bills, upkeep of the yard and grounds, mooring and storing a boat or other toys (jet skis, snowmobiles) and maintenance chores inside and out.

You also may need to consider expenses for the services of a local caretaker or property manager, laundry and cleaning, replacement parts and materials (and the labor to fix problems or damage), snow removal and other odd costs. Tips for reducing your ongoing maintenance, utilities and related costs are discussed in Chapter 7.

The ratio of time spent in a vacation home and the associated annual maintenance costs often drive owners to consider renting out their second home to help replenish the money pit. However, as discussed earlier, treating your vacation getaway as investment property severely limits your freedom to use it and carries tax burdens and related implications that may, in fact, fail to balance what you spend to maintain your second home.

Insurance. Actually, insuring your property will begin the moment you take title or full ownership, and it will be an ongoing cost as long as your name is on the deed. Sure, eventually it will be included (and, therefore, will be somewhat invisible) in your monthly mortgage payment, but insurance costs still warrant consideration in your budget.

Of course, on raw land, title insurance is much less than full-blown homeowner's or property policies. But as you improve your land and take on debt for its development, the necessary coverage and premiums will increase.

As with loan terms for land purchases, construction and second-home mortgages, insurance premiums for vacation property are often more costly than for your primary residence—maybe even double.

Simply, the risks are greater with a vacation home. As an occasional or secondary residence, the house is generally (and logically) considered vacant most of the time. As such, roof leaks, vandalism, break-ins, wear and tear, wind and fire damage and other potential problems are less likely to be caught, corrected or discouraged in a timely fashion.

Courtesy Precision Craft Log Structures

The likelihood of extreme weather conditions, and a vacation home's proximity to emergency services can impact your cost to insure the property.

Insurance companies also are more aware of special and extreme risks associated with covering homes in remote areas—specifically higher exposure to the elements, such as wildland fires, coastal winds and corrosive sea air, flood hazards and potentially higher replacement costs in outlying areas, among other issues.

Insurance companies are more aware of special and extreme risks associated with covering homes in remote areas.

If you rent out your house, there's also a greater possibility of damage and replacement costs, accidental or not, as well as the cost of liability insurance for the renters—more reasons to avoid using your second home to generate extra income. Insurance companies therefore must hedge against such problems or hazards if they are to be covered in the policy, which translates to a higher premium.

Historically, insurance coverage terms and conditions (if not premiums) for vacation homes have been similar to those for primary residences. But given the increasing popularity of second homes in the last decade-plus, insurance companies are now more apt to offer or create customized policies for vacation or seasonal property.

51

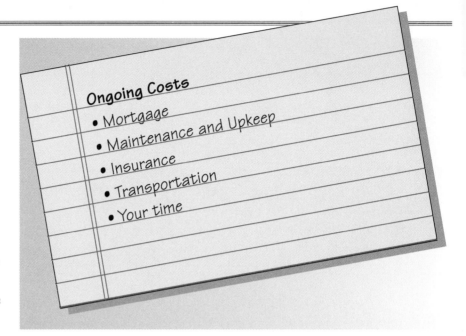

Ongoing Costs
- Mortgage
- Maintenance and Upkeep
- Insurance
- Transportation
- Your time

Ongoing costs are typically consistent monthly expenses, though your time commitment will likely vary depending on how often you use your second home.

For instance, your vacation home will typically contain less personal property, or less-valued contents, than your primary residence (so that's where the futon, your college dinnerware and grandma's console TV ended up). Because of this you may be able to reduce replacement costs for those items.

In addition, homeowner policies often contain (and charge for) living expenses should your home be destroyed. With a vacation home, however, you still have your primary residence in which to live, and therefore may be able to eliminate that particular clause in the policy.

Insurance companies may also consider certain protective or preventive measures that will elevate you from a "standard" to a "preferred" risk. Such provisions may include: security and fire systems wired to nearby emergency services (and even the home's proximity to those services); deadbolt and window locks, if not a more high-tech approach to security; the use of a local caretaker to check in on the place from time to time; proper or prescribed maintenance and materials that retard or bar fire spread or resist wind damage; and even having your second home within view of its neighbors. Preferred risk status through responsible care and use of your second-home property may, in fact, reduce your insurance premiums by 10 to 15 percent alone.

If you plan to enjoy some nearby recreational activities, you'll need to budget for them, as well.

Finally, consider (or ask about) upping the deductible on your second-home insurance policy (which will, in turn, lower your premiums), or leveraging a discount by carrying both your primary and secondary homeowner's insurance policies through the same carrier or underwriter.

Transportation and Other Expenses. Assuming you locate your vacation home within a few hours' drive of your primary residence, transportation will be a minor cost. Tack on food and cleaning expenses while you're enjoying your retreat, and it's a combined cost to be considered in the budget.

If you plan to play a lot of golf on vacation, consider a location and/or homesite on or near a golf course that offers an annual membership instead of paying per-round rates.

Such costs, of course, will depend largely on how often you use your second home. One four-day weekend a month probably won't cost you more than a few hundred dollars each visit (if that), even with the rising price of gasoline. However, if you plan to enjoy some nearby recreational activities—snow skiing, water sports, golf, tennis, etc.—you'll need to budget for them, as well.

If you purchase your lot and build your second home in a resort subdivision, however, some (or all) recreational and community service costs may be included in an annual homeowner's association fee. At my friend's cabin near Donner Lake in California, for instance, such dues allow "free" or discounted access to the adjacent golf course and a private beach on the lake, among other amenities for them and their guests or visitors.

The Value of Your Time

An often hidden or neglected cost is the time you'll spend throughout the planning, financing, design and building of your vacation home. Even if you outsource or hire profes-

As with spring and summer sports, consider the cost of enjoying your favorite winter recreational activities when calculating overall expenses.

sionals at every step, your responsibilities for the overall management of the entire process, including the maintenance and use of your second home, will require dedicated time on your part.

Of course, in rare cases, the effort and time you expend to create a dream retreat may not even feel like a burden or require any compensation beyond enjoyment of the vacation home itself—but it still costs you something. The price of your time is less a direct monetary calculation than a sacrifice of other activities, projects or payoffs, such as regular summer vacations with the kids, home improvements or starting a new business venture.

The price of your time is less a direct monetary calculation than a sacrifice of other activities.

To help gauge and schedule your time for a typical vacation-home project, treat it like money. Just as you would calculate how much you can afford to spend monetarily on a second home, do the same with your time on a weekly or monthly basis (see "Finding Free Time" worksheet, page 56).

Start with the baseline of 168 hours, the total number of hours in a week. Using the worksheet, figure in work hours, sleep time and other regular activities. Subtract that total from 168 and you have the amount of "free" time you can reasonably dedicate to this project. If you think it's not enough, you may need to adjust some of your other time.

Determining how much "free" time you can devote to your vacation-home project will allow you to make tradeoffs with other activities (at least for awhile ...).

As you move through the process, try to keep track of your time, as if you're billing it to someone, and compare it periodically to your worksheet calculation. Then, you'll be able to better adjust to the time demands of various stages of the process, more thoughtfully consider the value of hiring a professional or other help and appreciate just how much time a vacation-home project requires.

Using the worksheet to calculate your time, along with the other preparation exercises in this book, will help you articulate and document your expectations. When the going gets rough (and it likely will at some point), these worksheets will serve as reminders to keep you focused and perhaps even motivated. Who knows, they may even cause a much-needed chuckle during a stressful time.

Costs Versus Value

It bears repeating, especially after a discussion about the ongoing costs of owning a vacation home and value of your time to see it through: whatever you put into your vacation home, from proper preparation and planning to construction expenses and mortgage payments, the payoff is priceless.

Finding Free Time

Average hours spent at work per week

[total hours per day x number of days per week]: _____

Average hours per week commuting to work

[total hours per day x number of days per week]: _____

Average hours spent on work outside of the workplace (at home, business travel, elsewhere) per week: _____

Average hours of sleep per week [total hours per day x 7]: _____

Average hours spent per week on household or other necessary chores and personal duties (cooking, cleaning, eating, shopping, bathing, laundry, yardwork) [total hours per day x 7]: _____

Average hours per week on family duties (driving kids to activities/school, helping with homework, attending church or other activities, family obligations, etc.) [total hours per day x 7]: _____

Average hours per week for exercise: _____

Total obligated hours per week: _____

Total no. of hours per week (24 hours x 7 days): <u>168</u>

Minus obligated hours: _____

"Free" time per week total: _____

To be sure, it's easy to get sidetracked and lulled into thinking that the fruits of your labor might taste even sweeter if you rented it out and collected some income from it. Fight that urge. Even forgetting the tax and other financial implications of investment property, the freedom you'll have to enjoy your vacation retreat at your whim is invaluable.

If you need a reminder along the way, go back to the work you put into your Lifestyle Profile and vacation-home priorities, perhaps all the way back to Chapter 1 and the trilogy of primary considerations of convenience and comfort, proximity for short-term relaxation and ownership in something you created by your own imagination. Your focus is there if you need it.

Affordability

Now you know the costs associated with a vacation home, or at least the scope if not precise price tags. Here's the big question: How are you going to pay for them?

Finding Free Time — Sample

Average hours spent at work per week [8.5 hrs./day x 5]: 42.5

Average hours per week commuting to work [50 mins. total/day x 5]: 4.25

Average hours spent on work outside of the workplace (at home, business travel, elsewhere) per week: 5

Average hours of sleep per week: [6 hrs. x 7]: 42

Average hours spent per week on household or other necessary chores and personal duties (cooking, cleaning, eating, shopping, bathing, laundry, yardwork) [3.0 x 7]: 21

Average hours per week on family duties (driving kids to activities/school, helping with homework, attending church or other activities, family obligations, etc.) [2.5 x 7]: 17.5

Average hours per week for exercise: 6

Total obligated hours per week: 138.25

Total no. of hours per week [24 hrs. x 7 days]: 168

Minus obligated hours: 168

"Free" time per week total: 29.75

As with any luxury purchase, the cost of a vacation home should be calculated from your discretionary income. In other words, first cover the costs tied to your current home and lifestyle, and use what's left over for your second home. As stated above, you may have to sacrifice or wait on other luxuries or projects to free up money to pay for this one.

> *The cost of a vacation home should be calculated from your discretionary income.*

Whether you plan to pay for your vacation home in cash, out of savings or other assets, or finance all or part of the project, a simple calculation of what you can spend on a monthly basis will allow you to estimate affordability for your second home.

Most of us live on a monthly budget of mortgage payments, utility bills, food costs and fees or charges for lifestyle activities (though hopefully not paycheck to paycheck). Figuring how much discretionary income you have on that basis will, in turn, determine an affordable loan

You'll probably have to wade through a lot of paperwork to properly and completely calculate your budget and afford-ability.

amount for construction and mortgage payments, among other up-front and ongoing costs, on your second home.

What Others Spend

It may surprise you that 81.5 percent of potential second- or resort-home owners expect or are willing to spend less than $100,000 on a vacation home or other recreational property. More than half, in fact (53 percent), will spend less than $50,000, with fewer than 4 percent anticipating costs over $200,000.

Given that most potential recreational property owners plan to buy a single-family vacation home (as opposed to a resort condo or time-share), such costs appear fairly affordable for the typical, well-heeled second-home buyer.

A total up-front cost of $50,000 for land, design and completion of con-struction, for instance, works out to a mortgage payment of about $400 a month with today's relatively low interest rates and a 30-year term. It becomes even less if you purchase the land for cash (most likely you will) and pay off some of the construction loan before it is converted (or rolled over) to a mortgage loan (see "Financing," page 63).

Boosting Affordability

Can you realistically design and build a second home for $100,000, or even half that, including the cost of the land? Of course you can, and a nice one at that. While the price of developed homesites in the most popular vacation or recreational/resort areas, such as Myrtle Beach, South Carolina, Vail, Colorado, Taos, New Mexico and Lake Tahoe, California, among others, will eat up that budget, there are even more parcels within a 200-mile travel radius of your primary residence that are priced much lower, most with quaint small towns and recreational amenities nearby.

There's a widening range of options for designing and building your second home that helps reduce those costs (see Chapters 5 and 6) and thus boosts affordability. Purchasing a set of ready-to-build home plans, for instance, can cut your design costs by thousands of dollars, while kit homes and other factory-built construction options often shorten what home builders call "cycle time," or how long it takes to complete construction, which is often a more critical and expensive calculation than that of materials, equipment and other so-called hard costs.

In addition, many ongoing costs are less per month (and overall) than those you pay on a primary residence. Some, like insurance premiums, have been previously discussed, but you also can reduce your second

Design and construction costs may be reduced with options such as stock home plans and kit homes.

Photo by Northeastern Log Homes

Photo by Rich Binsacca

For rural homesites, where utilities may be difficult to tap, consider alternative energy sources and methods, as well as doing without some of the conveniences of your primary residence.

home's utility costs by lowering the thermostat when you're not there (though you'll still have a monthly cost for basic utility service). And, the energy used to fire up the stove, water heater and other appliances is curtailed by your occasional use of the property.

Telephone service, of course, is largely pay-per-use, with a monthly service charge for each line. When you settle on a location, or as you consider one (see Chapter 4), investigate whether you can use a cellular phone instead of requiring a standard line from a pole. Phone companies serving remote areas, in fact, are hip to building a cellular tower instead of a series of telephone poles.

If you can stand it, avoid dedicated Internet, cable, satellite and other non-essential services that are commonly the same monthly cost drain regardless of how much or little you use them. If you have to have such amenities, ask the various providers about pay-per-use contracts with discounted or waived monthly fees. Chances are, the overall costs based on your actual use will be lower than a standard monthly charge.

Remember, too, that you're using appliances and other finishes and fixtures, including floor coverings and furnishings, less often. In turn, that occasional use reduces wear and tear— and thus extends the usable life—of those items. And while popular resort and vacation-home locations often have a higher cost of living, you'll only have to pay the

Consider opening an interest-bearing savings account solely for second-home expenses.

difference during your stay rather than year-round. Some rural areas, in fact, might even have a lower cost of living than your primary residence.

The Value of a Budget

Calculating affordability on a monthly basis is useful beyond helping determine your eventual mortgage amount. Before that, your monthly discretionary budget can be used to pay off a land "loan" being carried by the seller (if full payment in cash is not your best option), cover property taxes and other up-front costs and fees, make improvements to the parcel, pay down the principal and cover the interest on a construction loan.

If there's a bit extra one month, consider opening an interest-bearing savings account solely for second-home expenses, or use the surplus to pay down a loan principal or balance.

It is impossible to say how much is enough per month to pay for a "typical" second home, start to finish. Rather, the costs are simply what you can afford. If that's $500 a month from now until the last mortgage payment on your vacation home, then the scope of your project, as well as its time frame from start to finish, should reflect that calculation.

Perhaps the most important use of your affordability calculation, in fact, is in setting a budget for design and construction.

Often, homebuyers are reluctant to reveal their budget, especially to a builder, preferring instead to gather bids or estimates on their blueprints and specifications. In that scenario, however, homebuyers often are surprised and dismayed by bids that are beyond their "secret" budget expectations. As a result, their dreams are sliced and shaved to bring the estimates down, thus souring the experience and even their eventual enjoyment of a second home.

To avoid that scenario, try the opposite approach: tell your chosen design and building professionals what your budget is up front, before the first line is drawn on the plans or computer, and stick to it. That way, they can produce drawings and build your house within that budget, be realistic about your choices of finishes and other products and have an important goal in mind throughout the process.

Tell your chosen design and building professionals what your budget is up front.

You can use your budget as a barometer to gauge the success of the project and those working on it. State your budget in the design or construction contracts as a "not to exceed" amount that, if exceeded, comes out of the builder or architect's pocket instead of yours. That's a sure-fire way to keep them motivated and on task.

Payback

Proper planning and smart savings obviously reduce costs and boost affordability. But, in addition, the interest on your second home's mortgage and some of the ongoing costs of your vacation home can be deducted from your annual income tax, assuming a total mortgage debt of less than $1 million and the home's use as a private, albeit occasional, residence (see "What the IRS Says," below).

While a tax advisor will be able to indicate specific deductions you may take, those to consider include association fees, property and other local taxes, closing costs and other mortgage, loan and title-generating charges. You may be able to deduct the cost of upgraded energy or insulation systems built into the home (called energy tax credits), as well.

What the IRS Says

Like it or not, the Internal Revenue Service (IRS) has significant say over how you use your vacation home. Your use, in fact, determines what the IRS will allow you to deduct from your income taxes which, in turn, impacts your affordability—not to mention your enjoyment of a second-home retreat.

Simply, if you need or want to fully write off items such as mortgage interest, property taxes, insurance costs and perhaps other fees and expenses per your tax advisor, avoid using your vacation home as income or investment property. The IRS then specifies your vacation retreat as a "personal use" home, suitable for year-round occupancy if not actually acting as a primary or permanent residence.

If, however, you decide to rent out your second home, be prepared for some complex IRS rules, as stipulated (and tightened) by the Tax Reform Act of 1986. For instance, if you lease out your home for up to 14 days in a tax year, you are not required to report that income on your taxes; rent it out for more than two weeks a year, and that income must not only be declared, but is taxable.

In addition, renting your vacation home for longer than a total of 14 days a year impacts your allowable use of the property. While you're expected and consented to conduct routine maintenance on the property, its status (according to the IRS) becomes that of investment property, with you as its landlord. Depending on the tax laws at the time, actually staying in your own vacation home for longer than two weeks a year may jeopardize or impact other deductions for maintenance and other property expenses.

From a customized homeowner's insurance policy to calculating a longer lifespan for a sleeper-sofa, there is significant potential to cut costs and increase the long-term affordability of your vacation home. Besides "freeing up" more money in your budget, thoroughly calculating affordability will mitigate financial surprises, better accommodate changes or delays and keep you and your builder on task.

Financing

Despite the fact that very few folks contemplating a vacation home will spend more than $100,000 (and most often less), that's a chunk of change that will likely require a loan. Your financing options, in fact, depend on the phase of the project you need to leverage, from purchasing land to paying on a mortgage.

Purchasing Land

A homesite purchased from a private landowner, or even in a developed resort subdivision, is most often paid for in cash. In some cases, the landowner may "carry" the land, allowing you to pay the purchase price in installments over time (as you would a lender), but most often the transaction is conducted in cash, in full, at the time of the purchase.

Photo by Rich Binsacca

A trip to the bank usually is typically found along the path to building your second home, though other lending options exist.

Why not get a loan for a land purchase? Simply, banks and other lending institutions hate to loan money for land, especially if it is a raw parcel, but even if it is developed or in a planned and approved subdivision. Without a house or other

Banks and other lending institutions hate to loan money for land, especially if it is a raw parcel.

high-value asset already in place, a homesite is a risky investment for a lender. If you fail to fulfill your loan obligation and the bank has to "take it over," foreclose, or otherwise assume the loan and ownership of the land, it will take time and effort to find another buyer. Lenders are not in the business of owning and selling land, and don't want to be.

Photo by Rich Binsacca

In many cases, a land purchase is negotiated and completed with a private owner without the need to involve a lender.

Even if you find a bank or thrift that will loan you money for a land purchase, chances are your down payment will be up to 50 percent of the sales price—the lender's hedge against a loan default—especially if the parcel is undeveloped. Lenders also will likely charge a higher interest rate and require you to pay off the loan in a much shorter amount of time than a conventional home mortgage, often less than five years.

Even with a higher down payment and interest rate, you'll also likely have to convince a lender that you plan to build on the parcel within a year or two, and perhaps even show steps toward that goal, such as preliminary construction documents or house plans. In short, the lender needs to be sure you will not only pay off the loan, but also eventually convert it to a mortgage loan, a much safer investment for the bank.

In fact, securing a conventional loan for a land purchase might not even make good financial sense. Unlike a mortgage loan on a house, the interest paid on land-only loans is not tax-deductible. In addition, taking on additional debt may hinder your ability to get a sufficient construction loan for your vacation home.

In fact, securing a conventional loan for a land purchase might not even make good financial sense.

There are, however, several options to help finance a land purchase outside the strict realm of conventional lending institutions.

The first is obvious: tap your savings or other liquid assets for the cash needed to buy the parcel. However, avoid raiding your retirement plan or other long-term investments or high-interest savings plans, which not only carry penalties and tax burdens for early withdrawals but cut your financial safety net even more than dipping into your personal savings. Leaving them in place also may help serve as collateral for a construction loan later on.

A general rule to using your savings is to do what's comfortable plus ten percent. Remember, you're investing in something of value (land, and eventually a house), which is likely to appreciate over the years, unlike a sports car or a ski boat. Therefore, some risk up front is appropriate. If you can anticipate big expenses or costs in the next year or so (or however long you think it will be before you start building the house), accommodate those figures into your planning, as well.

The primary benefit to using your savings is that it allows you to avoid assuming additional debt and thus boosts your ability to secure an adequate construction or mortgage loan for your second home. While lenders may look at your personal savings during their loan approval process, they'll more closely examine your long-term assets, income history and debt load.

If your savings and other liquid assets won't cover the price of the land, consider a private loan with the owner. As mentioned earlier, some landowners will carry the property and allow you to pay it off in installments (with some interest, of course). The landowner gains a steady stream of income and can spread out his tax burden on the sale over time. Unlike a conventional loan through a bank or thrift, a landowner may only require up to a 20 percent down payment (often less) and market-rate interest, with terms in the range of two to five years.

The major hitch in that plan is that you'll have to wait to build or otherwise develop the land. Most construction loans (which are generally easier to get than land loans) require proof of ownership, such as the deed and title insurance on the parcel—items you can't obtain until you pay off the landowner, unless you can negotiate their transfer or release before you make the last payment.

A third viable option for purchasing land is to take a second mortgage on your primary residence. Or, if you have enough equity built up and the interest rates are favorable, a refinanced first mortgage may free up enough cash (from your equity) to pay for the parcel. A major advantage to such loans is that the interest paid on them is tax-deductible (assuming an overall debt of less than $1 million). They also offer longer terms and market-rate interest to pay them off, making the entire project more affordable on a monthly basis.

Any new debt, however, whether private or conventional, will likely work against you as you move toward financing construction of your second home.

Construction Loans

While you may have the liquid assets or savings to pay for your home-site, chances are that the construction of your second home will require financing of some kind. Securing a loan, or the funds to build your home through alternative means, often is a detailed process that requires certain and several assurances to complete.

Chances are that the construction of your second home will require financing of some kind.

And, even more than a land loan, the terms of the loan are tight. Commonly, construction on a house takes less than a year to complete (often half that time), meaning that lenders, builders and other possible financiers will need to be repaid upon completion of your home—most commonly by a mortgage (or permanent) loan on the property.

Construction loans are based on very specific amount as defined by the building contract and other terms and conditions negotiated between you and your builder. Further detail is often required when applying for a conventional loan, as well as some other financing options. Essentially, however, a construction loan covers the cost of management, labor, materials, equipment and other expenses directly related to the building of your second home, and no more.

Typically, construction loans are secured in your name from a conventional lender or bank, or perhaps a mortgage broker. The money is doled out as needed and approved by the lender, to pay the builder and various subcontractors and suppliers upon completion of each phase of their work. As with a line of credit, you (as the debtor) only pay interest on the amount that's been released from the account.

Conventional Loans. Because there is still no asset on the property (and thus no desired collateral), lenders require a significant amount of detail before approving a construction loan, and may even require the builder to apply for or co-sign for the money (see page 69).

In addition to the deed to the parcel and proof of title insurance, lenders often require a legal description of the homesite (called a plat survey), completed construction drawings or blueprints, credit reports and a complete signed contract with a builder.

Most important, a conventional construction loan—whether secured by you or by the builder on your behalf—requires the approval of a permanent mortgage loan on the eventual home and property. While commonly secured separately, construction and mortgage loans are increasingly handled at the same time, saving time and money (see "Alternatives," page 69). Regardless, the approval or securing of permanent financing provides the ultimate assurance to the construction lender.

To further boost their confidence, lenders may also stipulate the blueprints be approved by the local or municipal building code authority, a process commonly called a "plan check," which often results in obtaining the necessary building permits (see Chapter 6 for further details). Unincorporated communities or areas usually do not have local building or plan check departments, however, relying instead on a county or state authority.

Photo courtesy Trus Joist

Loan programs for residential construction are well established, though financing for a second home is often scrutinized even more closely than for a primary residence.

Lenders also will take a close look at your contract with a builder. Simply, the contract needs to clearly and completely detail the material specifications, all cost estimates for materials, labor, equipment and other appropriate expenses, and a schedule of work and payments (called "draws") to the builder.

In addition, the lender will want assurances from the builder, whether in your contract with him or her or separately documented, about payments to subcontractors and materials suppliers—perhaps even requiring the builder to specify which ones he'll use on the project. The lender may even ask how the builder plans to obtain and forward copies of lien releases from each subcontractor or supplier, indicating they've

The release of funds and other administrative duties relating to the financial aspects of your project may be best handled by an independent third party.

been paid for their services and/or materials related to your house.

Releasing Funds. Lenders need this information for several reasons, but primarily to nail down the exact loan amount and determine how and when to release funds as the project progresses. Most often, the lender controls the disbursement of scheduled payments to the builder and watchdogs all or most of the key financial transactions and recording.

That responsibility includes making their own on-site examinations, independent of any municipal code or permit-related inspections, to evaluate progress and/or approve the release of funds based on a certain level of completion (or "phase"). Occasionally, you as the owner, can negotiate control over the money, but you assume similar responsibilities—and risks—along with that control.

Using a Third Party. Increasingly, and for a small percentage of the loan amount, the lender, debtor (you) and the builder agree to let a third party control the funds, removing any potential bias or delays and further assuring timely and accurate payments. In these cases, funds from the construction loan are kept in an escrow account and are issued on a voucher system.

Here's how it works: once the plumber, for instance, has completed his work, the builder issues a payment voucher to that subcontractor, who takes it to the third party authority where the construction loan is being held in escrow from the lender. The third-party company conducts an inspection to make sure the work has been done to everyone's satisfaction and according to the construction contract and terms of the loan. Upon verification and approval of the voucher, the company issues a check directly to the plumber and also collects a lien release for that contractor's work.

While this process removes a certain amount of control from the builder and you, it works well for everyone involved in the project. Lenders, for instance, are removed from inspection and verification chores and are reassured about the proper control of disbursement of funds. Home-owners are similarly assured that the funds are only going toward their project, and that the money is being allocated based on the home's progress, leaving enough to finish the job.

While using a third party removes a certain amount of control from the builder and you, it works well for everyone involved in the project.

Builders, meanwhile, are not asked to col-lect lien releases or disburse funds (which can be delayed or, in some cases, spent on other projects), while still getting paid for their work and expertise on a regular and reliable schedule. Subcontractors and suppliers also are con-fident of getting paid in full and in a timely fashion through the vouch-er system.

Some companies specialize in this type of service, but a title company, mortgage broker or private building inspector also can provide it. Such third parties, however, must be sufficiently bonded to be able to hold the construction loan in escrow and disburse funds.

Alternatives

As more folks decide to invest in a vacation or second home, the options for securing a construction loan or other financing have widened and become more flexible. In addition to conventional financ-ing through a bank or savings and loan, money for construction may be funded by a builder obtaining a construction loan on your behalf, tap-ping a builder's business line of credit or securing a combined "con-struction-to-permanent" loan.

Through the Builder. A builder may offer to secure a construction loan on your behalf or tap his or her own line of credit to finance the project. With either option, you may negotiate for the entire cost of con-struction or just a percentage of that estimated total, supplemented by your own assets, another private loan and/or a conventional loan.

When a builder applies for a construction loan on your behalf, in essence he's assuming ownership of the "house" until you take it over upon its completion under a mortgage (or permanent) loan. In fact, lenders may prefer to loan construction money and allow control of its disbursement by a reputable, experienced builder instead of a riskier

69

Photo courtesy of Pella Corporation

Completion and legal transfer of ownership (or title) of your vacation home triggers the conversion of a construction loan to permanent financing such as a home mortgage.

debtor (you). That said, you'll still be required to show proof of an approved mortgage loan before starting construction.

Another alternative is using a builder's business line of credit, in which "ownership" of the property is immaterial and there's no loan process to complete by you or your builder. Simply, the builder taps his own funds, essentially acting as the lender for your project. For his trouble, you not only pay for the time (labor) and materials charged to your project, but the interest on the outstanding balance of his line of credit applied to your house—which actually may have better terms than a loan you could get.

The primary benefit of using a builder's line of credit is simplicity. There's no haggling with lenders about your ability to repay a loan, nor the intrusiveness of that process. You are freer to negotiate a schedule of draws based on your affordability calculation, and it's unnecessary to secure a permanent loan on the property before beginning construction. With a building schedule, or cycle, of less than a year, however, you'll eventually have to get a mortgage loan to repay the builder and assume the debt he's accumulated.

The same freedoms gained by this method, however, also carry more potential risk. Without the inspection and disbursement processes required by conventional lenders, it falls on you to make sure that construction progress is in line with the budget. You'll also be solely responsible for evaluating the quality of the job and making sure it meets with your expectations and standards (or an agreed criteria) before making draw payments.

Where the Money Goes. When you agree to pay a builder directly, without the help of a lender or third-party, expect your first check or two to fund what builders often call "mobilization," or the establishment of his or her on-site operations (including dumpsters, porta-johns and basic utility service), as well as the first load of materials. These and all draws, in fact, should be tied to a specific purpose or phase of completion stipulated in the contract.

The last draw payment should be in the range of 7-15 percent of the total contract amount (if you've negotiated a schedule to repay the loan in full on your own), or the transfer to a mortgage loan that will repay the builder's debt. Regardless, the last draw should be held until the builder has secured a Certificate of Occupancy (CO) or other final approval by the governing building code agency. He or she should have all lien releases in hand, as well.

Because that final draw, or a portion of it, represents the builder's profit on the project, holding a percentage of the "loan" motivates him or her to complete the terms of the contract (and your house) to your satisfaction and get his or her ducks in a row before moving on to the next job.

Such terms may have to be negotiated if you finance construction privately, but are assured if you secure a conventional loan with permanent financing attached (as required in that scenario). In fact, no matter the financing source, builders may insist on proof of a mortgage loan to make sure they get repaid in full upon completion of work.

Builders may insist on proof of a mortgage loan to make sure they get repaid in full upon completion of their work.

Ask your lender and builder about so-called "construction-to-permanent" loan packages, which can reduce paperwork and transaction fees.

Construction to Permanent. An alternative gaining popularity among homeowners, lenders and builders is a construction-to-permanent loan. Because most conventional construction loans and some financing options require the approval of a mortgage loan, as well, lenders have begun to offer packages that cover both processes.

A construction-to-permanent loan takes care of everything up front, saving time and money in the processing of financial contracts.

Simply, a construction-to-permanent loan takes care of everything up front, saving time and money in the processing of financial contracts. In fact, the loan documents are the same, with shared closing costs and other loan origination and underwriter's fees, tax services and document preparation expenses—minus the delays when done separately. When construction is completed to everyone's satisfaction, a CO is issued, and a new appraisal of the improved property is conducted to reassess property taxes. The promissory note and deed of trust are then modified from construction to permanent loan status.

Among the parties involved, perhaps builders are the most reluctant to embrace construction-to-permanent loans. Tradition has a lot to do with their resistance, but more are seeing the benefits of this alternative—chiefly that allowing the homeowner to carry both loans eliminates the builder's financial liability to repay a construction loan or risk of not being repaid should he carry that responsibility.

In addition to obvious time and money savings for the homeowner, the conversion process also opens a window to "pay down" or pay against the loan principal, if possible or desired, which lowers the monthly payments. Another feature: in the case where the initial builder fails to complete the contract or project, the lender will take initiative to find a new builder to complete the job, knowing there's an asset to protect and wanting to convert you to a permanent loan as soon as possible.

Second-home Mortgages

Most people who build a vacation or second home will need to secure a construction loan and then a mortgage loan once the home is completed to finish paying the outstanding debt, as well as assessed taxes and homeowner's insurance on the property. If you financed the construction privately and in full upon completion, you'll still need to cover taxes and insurance costs, of course, but can forego the need to secure a mortgage loan.

But for the majority of folks, a mortgage loan is likely. Contrary to conventional wisdom, there's a difference between a "second-home mortgage" and a "second mortgage." The latter, in fact, is secured against property that already has a primary (or first) mortgage, as an alternative to a refinanced mortgage loan on your primary residence. A second-home mortgage, however, is a primary mortgage loan on a second piece of property, in this case your vacation home. As such, it is a completely separate loan agreement between you and a lender.

A second-home mortgage is a primary mortgage loan on a second piece of property, in this case your vacation home.

Of course, mortgage lenders are aware of the mortgage you're carrying on your primary home, which makes securing another first mortgage on your vacation home a potentially tougher process. You can grease those wheels a little if you've avoided any debt to finance land or any other expense, or high-priced and often financed purchases, such as a new car, a hot tub or kitchen appliances as you work through this process.

The Piecemeal Approach

A family I know owns some property in a wilderness area just outside of Boise. For nearly a decade, they've slowly but steadily built a vacation cabin on the parcel, doing most of the work themselves on weekends and holidays. As such, they have avoided a construction and/or mortgage loan, paying only the required annual taxes and insurance on the property. Eventually, the cabin will be completed, debt-free, for their enjoyment.

For my friends, the situation best suits their priorities: in their late 30s with two young children, the couple has a long way until retirement or empty-nester status, when they'll really use the cabin. Even so, the house can be occupied for weekend trips with the kids (during which time they work on it), thus serving its eventual purpose somewhat.

For whatever reason, whether you're unable or unwilling to secure more debt or can withstand a relative snail's pace until your second-home retreat is ready, the piecemeal approach is one alternative to achieving your dream. While progress may be slow, it's at a pace you can handle, and without the intrusion of a lender or other third party. If you've got the time (if not the money), it's something to consider.

As with some other financial considerations associated with a vacation or second home, your loan terms will likely be less favorable. Expect a higher interest rate, for instance, to cover the lender's increased risk. And, you'll likely be required to make a higher down payment, perhaps 30 percent. The length of the loan however, is still typically 30 years.

To lower your monthly costs a bit, consider an adjustable rate mortgage (or ARM), that will lower your initial interest rate below a fixed rate for a few years. At some point, when your ARM rate begins to creep past that of the fixed rate at that time, you may be able to refinance to a fixed-rate mortgage.

Any and all interest paid on a secured loan is deductible on your income tax, with some limitations mentioned previously. Make a careful calculation of your tax burden, given the additional mortgage interest and other allowable write-offs (see above) related to your vacation home, to further determine your affordability—a process your mortgage lender or broker may do, anyway, to help qualify you for a second-home mortgage.

FINDING YOUR PLACE

CHAPTER

FOUR

4

Photo by Rich Binsacca

Whether tucked away on a snow-covered mountain or on the shores of a sandy beach, the location of your vacation home should reflect your paramount wants and needs.

With a fistful of ideas and dreams in one hand, and a solid financial plan in the other, it's time to get out and actually find the location and specific site for your vacation home. This step represents an important transition, as all of your planning begins to manifest into the reality of an actual setting. In turn, the decisions you make at this stage will largely impact the design and construction of your second home.

Within this phase of the project, you'll make two key discoveries. The first is the setting, or location, of your vacation retreat, which concerns its proximity to your primary residence as well as the area's cultural atmosphere, services and recreational amenities.

The decisions you make at this stage will largely impact the design and construction of your second home.

The second discovery is the actual, buildable homesite within your chosen location or setting, with consideration for its proximity to a variety

75

of services and utilities, its accessibility by various modes of transportation, and other conditions that will, in some measure, dictate the structural and aesthetic features of your vacation retreat.

Finding a Location

Given that one of your principal considerations for a vacation getaway is that it is convenient and readily accessible from your primary residence, your choice of its general location is going to be within a reasonable drive of your home.

Natural beauty often plays an important role in determining the setting (and perhaps even the precise homesite) for your vacation home.

Specifically, that distance should be within a radius of 150-200 miles, or about a three-hour drive. Any more, and your enthusiasm wanes at the thought of a long trek for just a weekend's worth of rest and relaxation.

Much shorter, and you risk bumping up against or eventually being overtaken by suburban development that looks and feels just like home, thus dampening your ability to truly get away from it all for a long weekend or week-long stay.

In fact, within that radius you may already have an ideal location or setting in mind, or are at least aware of an appropriate or potential area. Living in Boise, I immediately think of in-state areas like Sun Valley, McCall, Stanley and Garden Valley, all of which are within a three-hour drive of my house. And while areas such as Coeur d'Alene, Idaho, and

Photo by Rich Binsacca

Park City, Utah are well-known resort and vacation hotspots in the Intermountain West, they are simply too far away for me to think of building a vacation home in either place—at least one I would use more than twice a year. In fact, most people who own second homes or simply vacation in those places are from or near Spokane, Washington, and Salt Lake City, Utah respectively.

Building Abroad

Occasionally, and often for very specific personal reasons, some folks opt to build their vacation home outside the United States or North America. One architect I know, for instance, designed a spectacular villa in Greece for a family whose primary residence is near Minneapolis; it turns out that the owners are of Greek descent with family living close to their new home. In fact, the house is a seasonal retreat (guess which season) and thus a bit different in its intention than a weekend getaway.

Building abroad, especially overseas, is almost always problematic. Land is likely to be more expensive, and codes and standards (as well as construction labor and supervision) are fickle, at best. Many U.S. architects hired to design homes abroad find another design professional in that location to help interpret local land-use, engineering and design regulations that may exist, as well as supervise the construction of the house given that constant travel from the U.S. is often inefficient and costly.

Construction methods and materials also are different; most foreign markets are used to building homes out of masonry products (concrete blocks) instead of wood or steel. While such materials may maintain the local aesthetic, the performance of the house may be less than what a seasonal occupant may be used to. Finally, even more so than a weekend retreat, a vacation home abroad requires a caretaker, as well as other maintenance and security measures.

The process of creating a vacation home within North America, however, is a popular choice among folks living within a short distance of the Mexican or Canadian borders. Crossing into those countries, especially Canada, is often no more cumbersome than building your retreat in the States, with similar building methods and standards.

If you're dead-set on a vacation home overseas, perhaps a more appropriate consideration is a timeshare or resort condominium, both of which allow you to avoid the lengthy, costly and often frustrating process of building a home outside of North America.

Drawing a Circle

Even if you think you're set on your location, and it's within the recommended radius (time and/or distance), take a moment to actually draw that radius on a map or road atlas. As an exercise, it will confirm your choice of locations, as well as point out nearby amenities or attractions. In addition, the resulting circle also will encompass every potential location, and probably reveal some of which you were either unaware or thought to be outside the circle.

To help exemplify this exercise, take a look at a road atlas or map of a well-known metropolitan area with a 200-mile radius drawn around it. It's remarkable, really, how wide that circle is on a map, encompassing most states (in the West), and entire regions, such as most of New England, depending on your starting point.

For instance, a circle around the Denver area wraps almost the entire state (the city being centrally located), thus revealing potential vacation-home locations up and down the Rocky Mountains and its vast foothills to the west. A similar radius around Philadelphia reaches about halfway across the state (the city being on the southeastern end), not to mention areas along the eastern seaboard, including Delaware and Connecticut. Possible locations near Dallas, meanwhile, include most of the lakes and national state parks that dot eastern Texas. I'll wager that a 200-mile radius around your hometown uncovers known and lesser-known areas to consider for your vacation-home location.

For some, remaining remote is a primary goal for a vacation home.

One caveat: Though you might be vacationing far enough away from the potential growth of your home city or town, consider also the growth patterns or predicted expansion of the location you are targeting, or perhaps a metropolitan area nearby. For some, remaining remote is a primary goal for their vacation home.

Narrowing Your Choices

Let's just say that your circle reveals three potential locations, one of which you are aware and perhaps familiar, the others less so. The next step is to schedule some time to visit and evaluate them based on your Lifestyle Profile and your other planning efforts, narrowing it down to the one for you.

Even if you are comfortable with a location, perhaps having visited and vacationed there before (as I am with Lake Tahoe and Sea Ranch from my childhood, and with McCall, Idaho, these days), your visits will be much more pragmatic and investigative this time.

Location	Percentage of Preference
Ocean beach	43.6
Mountains	26.9
Lake	23.3
Attraction area	10.0
Tropics	09.2
Golf course	06.0
Desert	05.0
Ski area	03.3
Source: American Recreational Property Survey: 1999; ARDA	

Second-Home Preferences
Your choice of vacation-home locations is obviously up to you, but it's interesting (if not overly surprising) to note that most folks prefer their getaways near water (an ocean or lake) or in the mountains. In fact, those three basic locations make up the vast majority of vacation-home preferences, according to the American Resort Development Association, indicating that the overall setting, if not specific activities, drive the decisions about where to build a second home.

Instead of napping all day in a hammock, as you may be on a "normal" vacation, you'll have your eyes wide open and radar up regarding the overall cultural atmosphere and specific services available—and become aware of the tradeoffs you may need to make if, in fact, you decide to build your vacation home there.

Small communities along popular attractions such as lakes and reservoirs often offer the services and other needs some folks require in a vacation-home setting.

Photo by Rich Binsacca

Photo by Rich Binsacca

If you're considering a given location, spend a good amount of time there, traveling the area and gaining a good feel for its culture and available services.

Stay Awhile

In selecting a location, you simply have to answer the question, "Can I/we live here for a week?" The only way to truly answer that question is, in fact, to live in a potential area for at least that amount of time.

Ideally, you should schedule a week-long stay during at least two seasons, most likely summer and winter, to properly gauge what the area offers, how easy it is to get there and get around, whether it's crowded, and what services are available. If seasonal changes are not dramatic enough to alter an area's access or services, go when you think you're most likely to vacation in your eventual second home.

A week in one place will provide enough time to properly experience the area and expose both its benefits and shortcomings compared to the vacation lifestyle you need and imagine. In all likelihood, you'll be forced to buy groceries or other supplies, look for recreational and other activities and events, and perhaps even search for and use mundane services such as a laundromat or an auto repair shop.

Take time to walk around town (if there is one) and discover what's there. Grab a local events calendar and see what festivals or local activities are scheduled during the year or season. See if there's a place that rents bicycles or other sports gear. Most important, try to get a sense of the local culture, especially if it seems to welcome newcomers or seasonal visitors. Most small towns are, in fact, friendly places—but there also

Photo by Rich Binsacca

Rural farming communities are becoming popular vacation-home locations for their charm and ambience (and lower produce prices).

may be an undercurrent of friction between those who live and work there year-round, and those who simply vacation there.

Mainly, however, you'll need to assess yourself and your mood throughout the week. Look for (and perhaps document) times when you feel inconvenienced or bored, unsettled, anxious or frustrated. By the same token, note times you feel truly relaxed and content, satisfied with whatever you're doing (or not doing) during your "vacation investigation."

Take time to walk around town (if there is one) and discover what's there.

Where to Stay

To properly and thoroughly evaluate a second-home experience and provide the most realistic environment, consider renting a single-family home or condominium (someone else's vacation retreat) in the area, as opposed to a hotel or motel.

From a practical standpoint, renting a home during your stay will probably compel you to find a grocery store or otherwise gather up supplies (or haul them with you from your primary residence or the nearest town on the way), thus evaluating what the area has to offer while providing a glimpse into the local cost of living.

Depending on the recreational activity (and its cost), consider the availability of equipment rental shops as an alternative to hauling your own gear to your vacation home.

Photo by Rich Binsacca

Of course, renting a house also gives you the strongest sense of the vacation-home lifestyle: of having an entire home to enjoy, fixing yourself a midday snack or finding a far-off bedroom for a quiet nap. My friend's vacation house near Donner Lake, for instance, has a generous kitchen, a pool table, a VCR (with an impressive stock of videos), and plenty of books and board games—not to mention more than one comfortable couch. In other words, stuff you'd never find in a hotel room in Truckee or even Lake Tahoe (or perhaps anywhere).

You'll also get a sense of what it will be like to care for and maintain a fully functional home-away-from-home. There's laundry, dishes, making beds and cleaning bathrooms, and perhaps some yard work and other periodic maintenance around the place. A weeklong stay in a second home will provide you with that perspective, as well.

Renting a house gives you the strongest sense of the vacation-home lifestyle.

Refining Your Plans
In addition to giving you a realistic sense of a second-home lifestyle, renting a house during your stay also will offer a chance to refine your

own plans and dreams for your eventual vacation retreat. Like test-driving a few cars before you buy one, you can get a sense of how you want your second home to live, what it will contain, how it will be finished and a host of other features and functions.

It may be, for instance, that you envisioned knotty pine kitchen cabinets for your own retreat, but after just a week of them in a rental house, you're already sick of that look. Also, consider the condition of the house you rent, the materials used to finish it inside and out (and whether they look in need of repair or constant maintenance). Take note of the water pressure of the faucets and toilets, as well as the effectiveness of the heating and cooling system. Is it a pain to keep a fire going or use a propane tank? How's the reception on the TV or radio?

The overall concept of your vacation home's design will likely be refined regarding both must-haves and must-avoids, after you spend some time in a rental home or two.

As with your evaluation of the town or area, take notes on your experience inside the house itself, specifically features you especially appreciated during your stay and those that fell short. Those impressions will go a long way toward making your vacation home a true retreat.

Tradeoffs

While creating an ideal vacation home is certainly possible, few areas will offer everything you want in a location. Most likely, deciding on a

Courtesy Classic Post & Beam

Photo by Rich Binsacca

Small towns may not have the big retail chains like back home, but they often have everything you really need for a long weekend or week-long stay, especially seasonal gear and equipment.

location often requires you to make some choices and compromises based on your priorities.

With your Lifestyle Profile as a guide, remind yourself about what's most important with regards to the location. Perhaps the little general store doesn't stock everything you can get at your supermarket back home, but the nearby recreational amenities are right up your alley. Maybe the secret's out on a place you thought was an ideal setting, making it too crowded for your tastes, even for a long weekend. It's up to you to decide how important those issues are in your vacation lifestyle.

While creating an ideal vacation home is certainly possible, few areas will offer everything you want in a location.

It's also critical at this point to separate your ability to overcome certain aspects of a given location versus simply overlooking them. Are you really willing to pack in all of your supplies to a truly remote alpine cabin (and pack out your garbage)? Can you insulate yourself in your second home from the bustle of a booming (and increasingly expensive) resort town? Maybe a one-hour drive to the nearest golf course or ski area was okay the first time because you were excited to get there, but it may become a burden as a regular routine on more frequent vacations in the future.

It will be tempting to rationalize that you can live with some inconveniences or little frustrations knowing that you'll spend relatively little time in the area. But the fact that you'll use your vacation home for relaxation (and a certain amount of recreation) makes it even more important to pick a place that allows you to set stress aside and have convenient access to the things you enjoy and need to feel comfortable.

Contemplating Retirement

As discussed in Chapter 1, it is common to consider your vacation retreat as a potential retirement home down the road. In fact, nearly half of all vacation homeowners foresee such a scenario.

On the surface, it seems logical, However, your lifestyle as a weekend retreater is quite a bit different than that of a retiree, and your choice of location (and your eventual second home) needs to accommodate both lifestyles if that's your intention.

For instance, ready access to emergency and medical care services may not be a high priority as an active adult, but may be critical after retirement and into your later years. Similarly, access to and around your home needs to be considered, from a paved and well-marked road to a house without steps or other potential hazards—which, in turn, may affect your choices of location

A week-long stay is one thing; a day-to-day existence is another.

and lot, as well as the home's design. In short, you may have to sacrifice an ideal homesite and certain features of your vacation retreat to accommodate a retirement lifestyle.

It may also be that certain amenities and activities that attracted you as a vacationer, such as snow skiing or water sports, become useless or unimportant in retirement. That said, if you imagine yourself fishing or playing golf during your long weekend retreats and in your later years, perhaps your ideal location can serve those needs through the transition.

Perhaps most critical, however, is that you must expand the basic question to, "Can I live here every day?" when considering the location or setting for your vacation/retirement home. A week is one thing; a day-to-day existence is another.

Again, at the end of your stay in a particular location, honestly answer the question, "Can I/we live here for a week?" If the answer is "yes," then you can confidently take steps toward securing a homesite and begin the design and building phases of your vacation-home project.

Toward a Homesite

After two weeklong visits to a location (or maybe even after just one trip), you'll hopefully have a good idea about the location for your vaca-

With any location, you'll probably have to make some tradeoffs ... though you should fight to be close to the things that really matter (like fishing, or whatever your passion may be).

tion home. In fact, use second or any subsequent visits, to investigate potential homesites, or the precise lot to build your retreat.

It's likely, especially if you rented a vacation home during your "location investigation," that you have some feel for what's available in terms of land and buildable areas for such projects within your chosen setting. You've probably seen signs or ads for real estate agents, land for sale, or perhaps new developments in the area.

Use second or any subsequent visits to investigate potential homesites or the precise lot to build your retreat.

Perhaps the most appropriate first step is to gather up local real estate magazines that show and list homes and land for sale in the area, and take them back home after your first or second investigative visit. Reading them will give you a fair idea of the market and gauge land prices for given acreages and features or level of development without the pressure of a sales pitch or the potential of a wasted trip. Such resources also provide insight into the real estate companies and land owners in the area, as well as giving you an even greater feel for the location you've chosen. Increasingly, the Internet may provide access to similar information, as well.

In the absence of such magazines or Internet content, or subsequent to them, contact real estate representatives in the area to inquire about available land or developed homesites. Agents will typically only represent the listings they have under contract, but also will show you any parcel upon request (in conjunction with the seller's agent, of course).

With that process, also ask about or look up the names of area lenders, insurance companies, architects, and builders and contractors. Local professionals are savvy about their market and the intricacies of vacation-home living. They may perhaps be more willing (or even able) to negotiate better terms and secure financing, customize policies, and design and build a home that best suits its location and site conditions as opposed to those back home.

Photo by Rich Binsacca

Depending on your preferences and needs, a homesite tucked out of view might be just the perfect location for your vacation retreat.

Settling on a Homesite

While Chapter 3 outlined the key financial considerations of purchasing land (and in doing so, delving into related issues regarding a parcel's state of development), other issues also will work into your decision.

Before you settle on a homesite simply because it's affordable and stubbed up for plumbing, you'll also want to consider any land-use, zoning and/or design regulations, views and exposure to sun and shade patterns (as well as neighbors), soil and other conditions of the parcel, and the relative access and reliability of utilities and other services to the eventual house. These considerations will, perhaps in large measure, determine the eventual design of your vacation home.

Land-Use and Design Regulations. As rural and other unincorporated areas become more popular vacation-home locations, local and municipal laws and regulations regarding land use are becoming prevalent.

While most rural or other potential homesites already allow (if not encourage) residential use, especially single-family homes, such land may be restricted from intruding on wildlife habitat or wetlands, utility rights-of-way, municipal road or service easements, or public lands.

Such limitations should be disclosed during the sale, but check them out and confirm them, anyway. If the sales contract does not include a professional survey, get one and have it checked and approved by the nearest land-use authority to make sure you properly identify the allowable building area on the parcel. Without such assurances, you face heavy fines (or worse, potential teardown) if your vacation home intrudes on restricted land.

While few argue the value of preserving public lands and wildlife, vacation and other rural homeowners often protest restrictions on the actual design of their homes. Ordinances and building code regulations may limit the size, height and perhaps even the color of homes built in wilderness or other outlying areas, especially if the location has become a popular spot for second-home construction—thus heightening the sensitivity to preserve a portion of the wilderness around it.

The point of such preservation action is to maintain the general look of the area and incorporate housing design and construction that is "tucked away" within it, causing as little impact on the aesthetic of the original environment as possible. While some homeowners squawk at such infringements, the concept of conserving the natural beauty of a given area—in spite of or at least in the face of development—is a noble pursuit that protects the value of your home as well as the environment.

Most vacation homeowners, however, are under the radar screen of these laws, which more often target large and obtrusive structures or resort complexes. Still, it pays to be aware of them as you (with or without a design professional) create your vacation home to mitigate any delays or fines in the code-approval or construction phases.

Exposure and Views. Another key consideration is the sun and shade patterns that pass over your intended building site, as well as its exposure to other natural elements and potential views to scenic vistas and your neighbors.

The ability to cut trees or otherwise clear the parcel for construction may be limited, thus creating a homesite that may be under a canopy of trees that will block or limit sunlight into your home or create potential hazards during snowfall or heavy winds.

Determining the sun and shade patterns will help "orient" or place your home on the parcel to maximize what exposures exist or can be created—capturing available sun in areas that need or appreciate it, such as a breakfast nook or a porch, or to supplement artificial light and heating sources. A limited amount of sun, for instance, may mitigate the use of solar or photovoltaic devices, while enough natural shade may allow you to reduce the size (and cost) of cooling equipment.

Capturing dramatic or desired views also will work into the placement and orientation of your home on its site. Certainly, a bank of windows and/or a long covered porch are appropriate means to view an ocean or lake vista, or perhaps a peaceful wilderness setting. But such exposures need to be protected with windows or other materials that maintain a comfortable climate inside the house, provide an adequate barrier to natural forces and maintain privacy from neighbors and passersby.

Before you build a vacation house with a huge bank of windows to capture a lush forest scene, for instance, make sure another house isn't slated to be built in that sight line. A panoramic view of the ocean is possible (and certainly desirable), but must be designed to withstand potentially high winds, dramatic climate changes, and the corrosive nature of sea air and moisture.

Developed subdivisions of vacation and second homes, often built on or near popular amenities (such as golf courses) offer certain advantages but also often impose important restrictions on design and land use.

Photo by Rich Binsacca

Existing Conditions. In addition to whether and what utilities and other services already exist on the parcel, you'll want to evalu-

Capturing views of natural beauty on your homesite should be a primary consideration in the final design and features of your vacation home.

Photo by Town & Country Cedar Homes

ate and document its overall conditions and features. In turn, this information will determine key components of the home's design and construction, such as the foundation and drainage system.

Beyond the homesite's "real" property (that is, anything permanently attached to it, such as an existing structure, trees and utilities), it's likely that the parcel also has been evaluated for certain conditions (much the same as a survey would specify its buildable area). Soils tests are common, as are data relating to the depth and location of the water table.

In fact, a comprehensive survey will likely include these tests, as well as a topographical map showing slopes and drainage patterns. Another possible test is for percolation, or how well the site drains or sheds water, especially in low spots.

As with exposures to view, sunlight and shade patterns, a homesite's general conditions, features and contours will need to be considered in the eventual orientation of your vacation home, as well as dictate in some measure the materials and methods used in its construction.

While the building pad on the site will likely be level (or made to be with earth-moving equipment), a good parcel will have and should maintain a natural (if not obvious) drainage pattern that helps shed water away from the home's foundation. A steep or sloping site, by contrast, will provide a watershed, but also will require more extensive (and costly) structural engineering to secure the house to the land.

A homesite's general conditions, features and contours will need to be considered in the eventual orientation of your vacation home.

Another key consideration is access to the homesite. Most commonly, there's a paved or perhaps gravel road leading to the parcel. If not, you may have to get a road cut yourself, which will likely require municipal approval, a permit and inspections. Least likely is a parcel that is forbidden to have road access, to which you'd have to hike in from the nearest road or parking area.

Assuming there is (or can be) a road right up to your homesite, you'll also want to consider its accessibility during inclement weather (snow,

The existing conditions of your chosen homesite will, in large part, determine the design of your vacation home and its surrounding landscape and other features.

Photo by Rich Binsacca

ice or rain), and if there is a service to clear and maintain it. Is it a private road or on the municipal map? The answer to that question will determine who is responsible for the road's maintenance and repair.

Existing Services. In Chapter 3, and again in this chapter, we've discussed the importance of determining what utilities are in place or available to service your vacation home. Ideally, the basic services are placed (or stubbed up) at the edge of the parcel, waiting to be connected to your home's meters and service panels. If not, you'll have to determine the services that are available and consider the cost to bring them to your homesite.

There's another issue to confront, as well: the reliability and performance of utilities and other services. Outlying and rural areas are often the last to upgrade their services, lacking both the demand and funds to do so in a timely manner. While there's not a whole lot you can do to speed that process, make yourself aware of the reliability of your utility services to properly establish your expectations for their performance—and whether you can live with those limitations or inconveniences.

If it appears that your basic services may be unreliable, or at least inconsistent in their performance, look for alternatives and supplemental means to make up the difference. As discussed earlier, small-scale solar or photovoltaic systems can store electricity for use during power outages, while a dedicated (on-site) propane tank or firewood may fuel a secondary heating source to an electric furnace. Maybe a satellite dish is a better TV signal receptor than a roof-mounted antenna. Perhaps a well is in your future.

Toward the Design Phase

With your location selected and your homesite secured, you've made the transition from concept and planning to the design and construction phases of your vacation-home project. Your design and building professionals, whoever or whatever they might be (see Chapters 5 and 6) will appreciate the effort you've made to gather information about the site, as well as your comfort level with the setting and existing conditions.

With your location selected and your homesite secured, you've made the transition from concept and planning to the design and construction phases.

As you move to the next phase, you will, perhaps for the first time, be working with someone else to make your plans and dreams a reality. Regardless of how you decide to design your home, whether with an architect or a home plan service, you must take the lead in making sure you get what you want.

Photo by Rich Binsacca

Vast parcels of land do exist in some of the most spectacular areas of the country. You just have to be willing to look outside the box of resort area brochures and web sites.

Be aware that no one will bring as much passion, interest and emotional investment as you will, and that such emotion will be both a blessing and a curse as you move forward in the process of creating your ideal vacation-home retreat.

93

DESIGNING YOUR HOME

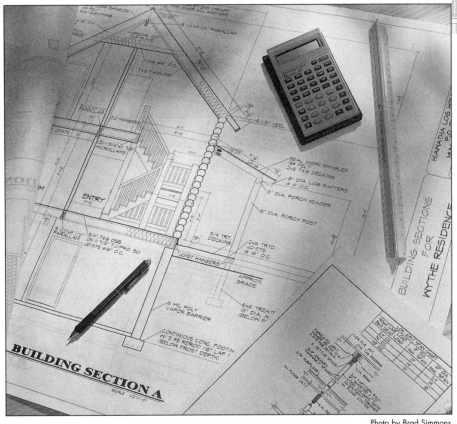

BUILDING SECTION A

*Several options exist
to help you create a
complete set of design
documents for your
vacation home.*

Photo by Brad Simmons

If you're like me, you look forward to the creative process, the act of
conceiving and refining something from nothing, no matter what it is.
But whether you're thrilled or intimidated by the prospect of designing your vacation home, and question how much you want to or can be
involved in that process, there are ways to reach your comfort level and
match your budget.

Gone are the days when hiring an architect was your only option. While
a full-service architect may, in fact, be the best choice for your situation,
there are several viable alternatives available: specialized design professionals, stock home plans out of a catalog, do-it-yourself design software, or a design-build firm.

The design process should consider everything, from materials selections to views and lifestyle issues.

Photo courtesy Town & Country Cedar Homes

This chapter outlines those options in terms of cost, services, benefits and appropriateness to your situation. You'll also gain some insight into the design process, from initial schematics to full-blown construction documentation and the first stages of selecting a builder or contractor. Finally, you'll discover some tips about what to include—and leave out—of your vacation home design.

Preparation

The more preparation you do before creating a vacation-home design, the smoother and better the process will go—resulting in a second home with lasting value in terms of comfort, convenience and enjoyment.

In fact, you've done most of the prep work already. But before you (or anyone) puts pencil to paper and draws that first wall of the floor plan, make sure your ideas and thoughts are organized. A good exercise is to go through your Idea File and other notes and categorize or separate them into rooms of the house, as well as indoor and outdoor finishes and other aesthetic and practical considerations. In addition, refer back to your Wants and Needs Lists (Chapter 2), which will help you and your designer (or design service) prioritize your thoughts.

Don't worry if ideas and priorities appear to conflict, or if certain finishes and details clash. The goal at this point is to bring a highly organized level of your concept to a design professional or service, which makes translating your prep work into a specific floor plan, elevations and list of specifications easier and faster.

To be sure, you will likely go through a few iterations of the plan, refining it toward the actual drawings and specifications (or products, systems and other details) used for the home's construction. But the more information you can provide up front, the closer initial drafts of the plans will be to your vision and expectations, and the more confident and satisfied you'll be during the design process—regardless of how you proceed in that endeavor.

Design Options

As mentioned before, you have several design options available, from a professionally trained and licensed architect to stock home plans and even design-it-yourself computer software. Your choice of a design path depends largely on your comfort level, needs and budget.

> *You have several design options available, from a professionally trained and licensed architect to stock home plans.*

Comfort Level. Your comfort level determines the amount of emotional support you'll need during the design process. If you are a neophyte to residential architecture and home building, and have very little experience or interest in the creative process, you'll likely gravitate toward a full-service architectural or building design firm that can guide you through both the design and construction phases of the project. But if you see yourself leaning toward the other extreme, you may just need someone to check your work as you go, offer some professional insight or help you solve a specific design problem.

Needs. Your needs will help dictate the specific type of design professional or practical services you require for your vacation-home project. It could be that you're comfortable with the design process, but less sure about hiring a builder and could use some guidance or a referral. If your second home is located in a remote or rural location and your availability is limited, perhaps you simply need someone to keep a diligent (and educated) eye on it during construction. Or, it may be you just need a licensed engineer or architect to stamp your plans before you submit them for plan review at the local building department. Simply, define the areas you think you might need specific professional services.

Budget. You already know how much you can (or should) spend from the work you did in Chapter 3, so now it's just a matter of matching that budget to the design services you want and need. Remember, however, that design fees are typically not covered in a construction loan (in fact, you'll likely have to show finished plans before you can secure such financing), so the money will have to come from other sources or means.

That said, there are more creative and competitive financing options for architectural design services, from per-hour and line-item services (as opposed to lump-sum contracts) to waiving design fees altogether in some design-build scenarios. Generally, however, the more you need from a design source—both emotionally and practically—the more it will likely cost.

Design Choices

Once you've got a handle on your emotional and practical needs, as well as your budget, it's time to consider your choices for hiring or obtaining design work. While several alternatives exist, they can be narrowed to four basic categories: design professionals; design-build firms; home plan services and kit homes; and do-it-yourself programs.

Design Professionals

Experience designing vacation homes is a key consideration for hiring a design professional to assist with your project.

Design professionals run the gamut from full-service architectural firms to building designers and draftspeople, from someone with a wealth of education and training to carry a project start to finish, to a person primarily with technical drawing skills and limited design perspective.

Photo courtesy Precision Craft Log Structures

Architects. Among this varied group of design pros, architects are the most well known. By education, training and professional licensing, architects understand the entire spectrum of structural, mechanical, and spatial relationships, building code compliance ("stamping the plans") and land use and other conditions of the chosen homesite in relation to the final structural and aesthetic design.

With such deep resumes, most architects are willing (and professionally able) to tackle a variety of projects, from commercial and civic buildings to a single-family home. As such, the majority of architectural firms are prepared in terms of staff and technical capacity to attract and complete large and varied design projects, requiring a substantial investment in people, equipment, marketing and sales efforts and other expenses.

In fact, relatively few architects are dedicated solely to residential design work, especially single-family homes for individual clients. Those with varied portfolios often view residential design (specifically single-home proj-

An architect's wide range of expertise, skill, knowledge and services is a blessing and curse in the design of a vacation home.

ects) as enjoyable diversions from their other, larger jobs—the chance to work in a relatively small and simple context to showcase their personal skills and style.

Even most successful residential architects tend to focus on larger housing-related projects, such as producing model homes for new subdivisions being built by production (or tract-home) builder clients. Others make their money selling stock home plans from their personal libraries or home plan resources, or by designing apartment buildings and condominiums, resort complexes, or huge luxury homes with budgets as big as their square footage.

An architect is perhaps most skilled in looking at "the big picture" and considering every nuance of the design process.

Architect Pros and Cons. An architect's wide range of expertise, skill, knowledge and services is a blessing and curse in the design of a vacation home. Few other architectural design professionals or other resources can bring a similar kind of comprehensive vision to a project and also carry it from the earliest stages of design through comple-

tion. But much of what professional and licensed architects bring to the table is overkill for a house design, especially in the context of a relatively simple vacation getaway.

As a designer, an architect's job is to articulate your ideas and preferences into cohesive floor plans and elevations through a progressive refinement of initial schematic drawings to the final documents used in construction. You should see your vision of a vacation getaway come into focus, with the elements, spatial relationships, finishes and details expressed at the beginning of the process integrated in the home's eventual design. In short, an architect pulls your prep work together and draws your vision, even if you hadn't yet fully imagined it.

An architect pulls your prep work together and draws your vision, even if you hadn't yet fully imagined it.

In addition, you should expect an architect's work to be technically accurate and comprehensive in its list of specifications based on what the house requires as well as your preferences and needs. Nothing should be left to chance or debate on the job site; the plans should offer a clear road map for the builder and subcontractors to follow. (For insight into how architects and other design professionals and services help you read and understand construction documents better, see "Beyond Blueprints," page 103).

As a licensed designer in your area (often a state designation), an architect can facilitate the plan approval process, in which the local building authority checks the plans for code compliance, structural and mechanical provisions depending on the home site or surrounding community and other details related to occupied structures—thus triggering a permit (and related fees) to begin construction.

Beyond his or her design work, a professional and licensed architect may act as your liaison with the builder, often helping suggest, screen and select the right contractor for the job and then staying on to coordinate and supervise some of the home's construction as your advocate.

That litany of architectural design and consulting services, however, is more typical of a larger, non-residential project than what's often required for a single-family vacation home. And because few architectural firms focus solely on housing, much less vacation homes, they offer more services and levels of detail than you may need or can afford.

That fact alone, in large part, helps explain why a full-service architectural firm may charge up to 15 percent of your overall construction budget in design and related service fees. For example, within a $125,000 vacation-home project, an architect's design fees may be nearly $20,000, leaving a hair over $100,000 to buy materials and pay the builder.

In addition to paying top-dollar for services you could get elsewhere for less, or simply don't need, an architectural firm may push your project down the priority ladder in deference to larger and higher-budget work, causing delays and blown expectations regarding the service and attention you get from your design professional.

Lastly, and again because so few operate in the ream of a single-home project for an individual client, architects are notorious for going over budget. Generally unfamiliar with the range and prices of residential products and systems (as opposed to those for larger, non-residential projects), and also wanting to specify only "the best" in their design projects, some architects underestimate the cost to actually build

Photo by Brad Simmons

Computer-aided design, or CAD, has made it easier for design professionals and their clients to communicate effectively.

their designs and fulfill the specifications. When a builder or contractor provides a more refined cost estimate based on those plans and specs, you may be faced with a beautiful home you can't afford to build.

Hiring an Architect. You wouldn't hire a personal injury attorney to defend you in a custody case, so if you're set on hiring an architect, look for one with experience designing vacation or second homes. Even more specifically, look for a design professional familiar with the area in which you plan to build your getaway, as the conditions and requirements for a home on an ocean cliff

If you're set on hiring an architect, look for one with experience designing vacation or second homes.

or steep lakeside lot are quite different than those for a cabin set in an alpine meadow.

In addition, consider an architect willing to offer his or her services separately or progressively. To capture single-family work and still make a profit, some savvy architects (and some full-service firms) have taken to billing for their services in piecemeal form instead of as an overall package. As a result, they are often able to better define the scope of their work and set more accurate budgets for their clients.

Finally, look for a design professional you like and can envision working with over the course of at least a few months, if not longer. You can expect frequent contact and conversations with your architect, and the two of you need to be in synch to successfully complete the design to your satisfaction. Personality, therefore, is as important as design skill and relevant experience. Discount or ignore that aspect, and you'll likely end up bumping egos and expectations with your architect.

Unlike builders and contractors, who are historically hired in a bid situation, architects and other design professionals are hired for a single-family home project on the basis of a negotiated contract. This process allows you to investigate and create a list of appropriate architects (or firms), interview them with regard to their relevant experience and interest in your project (as well as their personality fit), and negotiate fees and a reasonable payment structure. (For more details, see "The Design Contract," page 108)

Building designers usually bring a more relevant and dedicated expertise to a vacation home project.

Building Designers. In contrast to most architects, building designers are typically unlicensed professionals with less formal education and training in the broad spectrum of architecture and engineering. That said, many have developed an excellent design sense and skill and are often focused on single-family homes for individual clients. The result: building designers usually bring a more relevant and dedicated expertise to a vacation-home project than a typical, full-service architect.

So how is it that building (or home) designers can make a living in a realm that most architects avoid because of skimpy budgets and razor-thin profit margins? Simply, most home designers choose to focus on housing and smaller-scale projects rather than go after larger jobs—and all of the overhead and staff required for such work. Also, home designers dip into other areas of the residential realm, such as remodeling and interior design, to supplement new-home projects.

Beyond Blueprints

Reading blueprints—the roll of blue-hued construction documents found at every job site—often causes a disconnect between clients and design professionals. Simply, non-designers are unaccustomed to viewing things, especially a house, in the two-dimensional form of a floor plan or elevation rendering at ¼-inch scale. It's difficult to decipher spatial relationships, much less visualize a view from a window, when the walls are mere lines on a flat page.

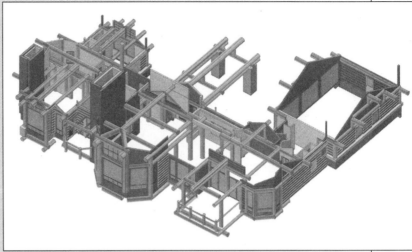

Design and rendering courtesy Keven McKee Associates

With the advent of computer technology for architectural design, called CAD, architects and designers have been able to better articulate their 2D plans into three-dimensional models "built" on the computer and printed out for client review. As a perspective (or axiometric) view, the floor plan and elevations literally rise off the page or computer screen, giving clients a better and truer sense of dimension.

Sophisticated versions of the software even allow virtual tours, or VRs, which literally (if virtually) walk a client up the walk, through the front door, and around the house. Designers can also program the path of the sun (to show shade and exposure patterns), integrate real views and landscape from digital photos and specify and show finishes inside and out.

Not all design professionals have this capability in-house, and those that do often (and justifiably) charge extra for the computer time required to create CAD models and VRs. But the software is becoming less expensive, and many design professionals see the technology as a necessary element to sell their skills as well as help their clients better understand and appreciate their work.

Most of a building designer's job is the design work—producing the plans for construction. However, because most designers focus on housing, they typically have a network of builders and contractors with whom they are familiar. As a result, designers (like some architects, and perhaps moreso) can assist you in selecting an appropriate builder for your project, and perhaps act as your liaison during construction.

Building Designer Pros and Cons. The knock against building or home designers is that they are unlicensed, which means they need to subcon-

Photo by James F. Wilson

*A good working relation-
ship between your design
professional and the building team is essential to a
successful project.*

tract with an engineer or other licensed design professional to submit
their plans for review at the building department on your behalf, or
defer that task to the builder.

In addition to simply getting someone else to officially "stamp" their
plans, many (but certainly not all) home designers may lack the professional training and skill to calculate and design complex engineering or
architectural details, which may be required for a home on a sloping
lot, with an extreme exposure (such as high-wind and coastal areas) or
in suspect soil or other site conditions (such as a seismic zone).

That said, building designers are, like remodeling contractors, increasingly conscientious about being considered and respected as professionals among their clients. To achieve that status, a growing number have
joined and become certified through the American Institute of Building
Designers (AIBD), among other professional organizations. Though not
limited to home designers, AIBD has a decidedly residential focus, with
many of its educational and certification programs geared toward the
housing realm.

Certification through AIBD and other organizations provides building
designers with a wider perspective, especially in such areas as how to

run a successful business, marketing and sales, estimating and building code issues. However, certification is not a license; as such, AIBD and other programs or groups make no assurances nor particularly watchdog their members.

The greatest upside of hiring a home designer is that most are focused on single-family home projects and are therefore intimate with the proper scale, scope and costs of such work. Their budget estimates are often closer to the target and they can more successfully marry your dreams to a realistic cost than a typical architect can. A new house also is a high priority for home designers, commanding their attention and dedication, and resulting in a higher level of service and satisfaction.

Because most building designers are small or one-person businesses, with little overhead and other expenses outside of perhaps a small office space and basic equipment, their design fees are typically less than an architect or full-service firm—up to 10 percent but perhaps as little as 5 percent of your construction budget. With the same example used for architects (see above), you may have as much as $115,000—an extra $10,000 or so—for the building phase of your project if you contract with a building designer.

And, as mentioned earlier, many designers work closely with (or even for) builders and contractors, giving them an excellent perspective on

Computer modeling, used increasingly by design professionals, helps build your confidence in the design process.

Design and rendering courtesy Keven McKee Associates

which builder might be best for your project, or perhaps partnering with a contractor in a design-build scenario (see page 108).

Hiring a Building Designer. As with an architect, finding the right building or home designer is mostly a matter of proper fit. Sure, most building designers focus on housing, but your selection process should delve deeper. Diligently examine a designer's portfolio of past projects, both verbally and visually, to gain an understanding of his or her prevailing style and comfort level with your type of project.

In addition, be clear about what you want from your designer in terms of design work and other services, if necessary, and whether that person is capable of meeting your needs. Also, ask about how plans are stamped and submitted to the building department, how complex engineering is accomplished and the value of any certification or other professional designations. In addition, query their workload and where your project fits in their schedule and among other priorities. And don't forget to ask about fees and payment structure (see "The Design Contract," page 108).

As with any design professional or service, try to find a compatible or complementary personality to your own.

And, as with any design professional or service, try to find a compatible or complementary personality to your own. If an interview morphs into an easy (yet productive) conversation, take it as a good sign that you can work closely with that designer for at least a few months. Settle for a suspect fit on this particular score, and you'll most likely end up souring on the process.

Draftspeople. Among the range of design professionals, draftspeople are the least design-oriented. They are known and relied upon more for their technical knowledge and drawing skills. Still, they may be your best option, and certainly one of the least expensive among this group.

Draftspeople, especially those hired for housing projects, may work on a freelance basis or independently within the context of a larger design firm. More often, however, draftspeople for residential projects work independently on a subcontract basis for other design professionals, home builders and contractors, government agencies, and homeowner clients. (One guy I know is a fire department captain by day, a for-hire draftsperson by night, generating plans for small licensed contractors and remodelers to submit for permit.)

Some draftspeople supplement their incomes as plan checkers for the local building department, or by providing tenant improvement sketches and plans for small businesses and building owners. Increasingly sophisticated in the use of computer design and drafting (CADD) software programs, draftspeople are often technically and technologically capable of working with a variety of clients.

For most of their projects, however, the mission is clear: to refine schematic or initial design sketches into architectural plans and details that can be evaluated and perhaps stamped or submitted for permit by a licensed design or building professional.

Within that scope of work, a draftsperson may be hired to manipulate or slightly alter stock home plans (explained later in this chapter), and may also address any site-specific or engineering details not included on a set of stock plans. For instance, a draftsperson may move a few walls, expand the kitchen or master bedroom, add a deck or perhaps even specify and detail a more extensive foundation structure on a set of standard vacation-home plans you purchase, either from a stock plan service or kit home manufacturer.

For that work, a draftsperson typically charges by the hour (probably in the range of $100 per), or perhaps on a flat fee basis. And, his or her fee is in addition to any other design costs you may have paid to an architect, home designer or other design source to produce sketches or an initial set of house plans.

A complete home project, in fact, is probably over the head of most draftspeople. While technically capable (perhaps even moreso than a building designer), a draftsperson typically lacks the design skill and savvy, as well as the necessary comprehensive vision, to articulate your concepts into a cohesive plan and list of specifications.

In some instances a talented designer may hire or partner with a draftsperson to refine his or her initial drawings of your plans, thus supplementing the designer's lack of technical skill.

A talented designer may hire or partner with a draftsperson to refine his or her initial drawings of your plans.

Hiring a Draftsperson. Some architectural and design firms may offer the services of an in-house draftsperson to help you complete or refine your project (such as altering a set of stock or computer-generated home plans). More often, however, draftspeople work independently or on a freelance basis, making them harder to find than architects or building designers.

As with those folks, look for a draftsperson with relevant experience in the services you require, such as altering some previously designed plans or simply refining a set of sketches or a particular design detail. With that consideration, try to work with a draftsperson with some experience in vacation or second homes with similar site and location conditions as your project, who may yield some insight into a technical aspect of its design and construction.

Given that a draftsperson's job is typically short-term, a personality fit is less of a concern, though you certainly should avoid someone with whom you are uncomfortable or lack confidence.

The Design Contract

Once you've selected your design professional, the contract should reflect every detail and expectation of their services and related responsibilities, ideally with a cost attached to each task (instead of an overall fee). The scope of work, either overall or in phases, should be clear and agreed upon by everyone at the table.

In addition to agreed fees, the contract should include a clause that holds your design pro accountable if he or she should create plans and specifications that exceed your budget for construction—such as a penalty or refund, fee discount, or free revisions to properly align the design and budget.

(That said, you also have a responsibility to keep the budget and fees in line, such as avoiding additional or excessive revisions of the design work and tempering your tastes and selections in terms of finishes and products. If necessary, refer to your planning exercises as a reminder of your priorities to help keep you on track).

In addition, the contract should spell out specific deadlines for the typical stages of design and other services, from initial schematics to the final working drawings and beyond, which also will serve to determine the payment schedule at the completion of those stages. Set deadlines for the selection of a builder (if part of your architect's services), as well as the beginnings of a construction schedule—at least a target date of completion.

Design-Build

A design-build scenario is relatively new to home building, spawned from the residential remodeling industry to simplify the processes by combining the responsibilities associated with home design and construction under one roof.

The most common forms of design-build are either as an informal or per-project partnership between a design professional and a building contractor (each with their own independent businesses) or in the structure of a single firm that offers both design and building services.

Either way, the over-riding goal is the same: to leverage the skills and experiences of each party (design and build) in order to streamline the entire process and keep costs in check. And design-build firms—formal or informal—are often focused solely on housing, thus offering the proper perspective and providing the appropriate services to address your needs.

Periodic on-site meetings among the design-build team often mitigate miscommunication, delays and cost overruns, allowing the job to run more smoothly.

Design-build is often especially favorable for vacation- or second-home projects, where coordination between the budget and the final plans, as well as the design and construction phases, is often most critical considering the typical homeowner client's comfort level, financial commitment and personal involvement in the process.

How it Works. Precise operations vary, but generally a design-build firm or scenario works this way: From the first meeting about your vacation-home project, you meet with both the builder (or a representative of that phase of the project) and the designer or architect. While the design pro will likely take the lead in refining your concepts and ideas into a formal set of plans, he or she relies on the building side to review and offer insight into the design process as it relates to eventual construction, as well as keeping a close tab on the budget.

By being a part of every conversation about the design, the builder can interject relevant insight into certain details or specifications along the way, and may be relied upon to make cost estimates regarding certain products or finishes within your budget. The designer, meanwhile, can focus on the design aspects of the project, knowing that someone with a trained eye is watchdogging costs.

A design-build scenario or firm eliminates the need to find and hire a builder to construct the house.

Photo by Town & Country Homes

The efficiency of an in-house design-build team is a significant advantage for many vacation-home projects.

For instance, while the designer may sketch or detail a certain aspect of the construction (such as deep roof eaves or cantilevered balcony), the builder can, early on in the process, review and evaluate that detail for the time and materials required to build it. If the detail is too expensive or too difficult to build, or can be built more efficiently with a few changes in its design (called "value engineering"), the process has eliminated or at least mitigated cost overruns, confusion and delays before and during construction. (In fact, most design professionals who work long enough in this scenario eventually gain a solid handle on the costs and construction issues associated with their design and specifications, making the process even more efficient.)

No More Bids. In addition to valuable and cost-effective coordination during the design phase, a design-build scenario or firm eliminates the need to find and hire—either by competitive bid or negotiated contract (see Chapter 6)—a builder to construct the house. Not only do you avoid the pitfalls of the bid process, but also you gain a builder's perspective from the beginning instead of introducing a new, if valuable, opinion after the bulk of the design work is completed.

Design-build—especially in the context of a single firm—also mitigates conflicts of ego and power between a truly independent design professional and builder, which occur most frequently as the project transitions from design to construction. As costs are refined and contracted, permits secured and ground broken on your vacation home, a cohesive relationship and clear understanding of roles and responsibilities between the designer and the builder will make for a smoother (and friendlier) process.

No More Fees? Historically, architectural and related fees in a design-build scenario were on the low side of those for an independent building designer (about 3-6 percent of the budget), with the homeowner client typically signing a separate contract for the construction phase.

Because the contracts were separate, clients had the option of paying for design services (resulting in a complete set of building plans) and then deciding whether to actually build the house or even hire the "build" side as opposed to putting the plans out to bid to other builders.

Understandably, design-build firms quickly grew tired of putting in design work on single-family home projects, collecting relatively small fees, and then watching their clients either shelve the project for lack of financing or interest, or worse, "shop" or bid out the finished set of plans in hopes of lowering the construction costs.

In those instances, the "build" side of the business is left to fend for itself, bidding on other jobs like a typical builder and thus suffering the slight margins and higher opportunity cost of that process. Meanwhile, the entire business suffers because, for the most part, design fees alone cannot (and are not expected to) sustain or support the combined staff of a design-build firm.

To combat that scenario, design-build firms are increasingly luring clients by promising to waive or discount design fees if the homeowners agree up front (via a letter of intent) to contract the construction phase through the firm. In essence, the firm is tossing out the $7,000 or so (often less) it would collect in design fees for the bigger carrot of a $100,000-plus construction contract.

In reality, the deal is a bit more complicated and varies with each firm. Even with the letter of intent to hire the "build" side, clients still often pay on an agreed schedule for design services during that phase of the process, albeit in the 3-4 percent range. Simply, paying for professional services makes it valuable in the mind of the client while generating some cash flow for the design-build business.

Paying for professional services makes it valuable in the mind of the client while generating some cash flow for the design-build business.

And, should homeowner clients become dissatisfied during the design process, they can still walk away—often with some semblance of a finished plan to refine and bid out elsewhere—while the design-build firm still makes some money to help sustain the business.

Once the plans are completed and the project moves into construction, some or all of the design fees paid to date are credited in a separate construction contract. For instance, if the client paid a total of $1,000 in

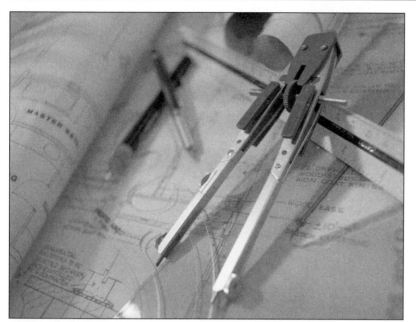

Ideally, a design-build scenario creates efficient checks and balances between the design and the construction processes, as well as smoothing the transition from one phase to another.

design fees, the construction budget would be discounted by that amount. Another option would be to waive the final design fee installment, representing perhaps 15 percent of the agreed design fees, once the construction contract is signed.

Few, if any, firms will provide a cash rebate for design fees, but some have been known to waive those fees up front as opposed to the back-end to the design phase. The problem with that scheme is two-fold: the design side feels rushed to generate plans so construction (and cash flow) can begin as soon as possible, while clients may take advantage of a "free" deal and feel at liberty to demand excessive alterations and revisions to the plan. The result not only belittles the value of design services, but also affects the quality of the work and the efficiency of the design-build scenario.

Not all design-build firms are in the practice of waiving or discounting design fees, but it seems to work for everyone involved. As the client, you pay for professional and arguably more reliable and accurate residential design work that is assured to meet your budget. The design-build firm generates some cash flow to support its design staff with the bigger cash cow of construction assured down the road to sustain the overall business.

(It should be noted here that home building, despite public perception, is typically a narrow-margin business. Most builders, in fact, make about 5-6 percent profit—a return slightly better than a basic money market account—on projects that last up to six months or more. However, the cost efficiencies derived from a design-build scenario, the result of fewer delays, change orders and cost overruns, help boost that thin margin without affecting the amount of your construction loan.)

Why Not Design-Build? Clearly, design-build offers several benefits and advantages in the creation of a vacation home, perhaps moreso than any other design option. There are, however, circumstances that may point you in a different direction.

For instance, using design-build (especially in the context of a single firm offering both services) may feel like you're putting too many eggs in one basket. You may feel a loss of control over the selection of the builder, pressured to sign a letter of intent of construction contract or be concerned about the quality of the design for such a slight fee.

If you look forward to the builder selection process independent of the design phase, with or without the help and counsel of a design professional, perhaps design-build is not for you. Similarly, if you're dead-set on a different design option, specifically stock home plans or a do-it-yourself program, the value of a design-build scenario is reduced if not eliminated. It also may be that you have an architect and/or a builder already in mind, neither of whom are affiliated with each other or another design-build scenario.

In addition, it may be best to hire a design pro or service near to your primary residence (see "Here or There?" page 114). Close contact with a designer or architect is arguably more critical than with a builder, with whom weekly walk-throughs and meetings are more the norm. If you want your designer here and your builder in the area of your vacation home, chances are a design-build firm cannot meet those needs.

Finally, as mentioned earlier, it's probably a good idea to avoid a design-build scenario or firm that offers to waive design fees up front. Chances are you'll be disappointed in the design phase, souring your excitement and probably affecting the overall efficiency of the construction stage and thus your ultimate enjoyment of a vacation home.

Hiring a Design-Build Firm. Hiring a design-build firm is a process of elimination and proper fit. If this scenario sounds like the right one for you, seek out friends or family members who have had a design-build experience; lacking that, check the local phone book or a large building products retailer or lumberyard (one that sells to contractors) to create a list of potential candidates.

As with an architect or building designer, narrow your list by investigating the firm's past work, especially regarding vacation or second homes. It may be, in fact, that the right firm for your project is

Narrow your list by investigating the firm's past work, especially regarding vacation or second homes.

located where you plan to build your second home (as opposed to near your primary residence), which is likely to have the best perspective for and portfolio of vacation-home projects (see "Here or There?" page 114).

Perhaps even more critically than with any other design professional, the design-build scenario demands you feel comfortable with the people you'll work with to create your vacation retreat. Start to finish, the process could take a year or more and relies on your involvement.

Therefore, plan to meet at least a few times with each design-build team on your short list of candidates. In addition to their relevant experience and client references, gauge their approach to the process, the steps they'll take in the design phase, coordination and assurances regarding cost control and the firm's fee structure.

Here or There?

Regardless of whether you think your best design option is an architect, building designer, draftsperson or design-build firm, a key consideration is whether to hire those services close to your primary residence ("here") or near the chosen location of your eventual vacation home ("there").

Perhaps the key determining factor in that quandary is a designer's relevant experience with second homes, especially if there are any conditions (such as high winds, waterfront property or seismic hazards) that are more extreme or different than in the area where you reside most of the year. In those cases, a design pro or service in the region of your vacation home will likely have more experience with those matters, as well as with local building codes and other regulatory issues.

A design pro or service who is "there" can also help supervise or at least watchdog the construction of your vacation home on a day-to-day basis, given that you are unlikely to visit more than once a week (and probably on weekends), if that often.

The obvious upside to hiring a design pro or service "here" is proximity. The design process, moreso than the building stage, most often feels like an "on-call" situation, where frequent meetings to review and discuss the progress of the plans are both planned and impromptu. Some folks feel more comfortable knowing they can bop down to their architect's office at a moment's notice (or vice versa) instead of having to take a day off to drive upstate for a meeting.

Computer technology, specifically the use of e-mail and the World Wide Web, has started to shrink the world a bit, including the architectural realm. It is increasingly common for clients and their design pros in different locations to communicate and share files electronically, reducing the need to make every meeting a face-to-face encounter; clients can review detailed drawings, either on a special web site or via e-mail attachments, and provide feedback to the designer. Computer wonks on both sides of the line love it, and it may someday eliminate the question of "here or there?"

Photo by Hearthstone Homes

Stock home plans and kit homes offer an increasing variety of materials and aesthetic choices for vacation- and second-home retreats.

Stock Home Plans and Kit Homes

The availability and increasing range of stock home plans and kit homes as a design option for your vacation retreat offer a hybrid between hiring a dedicated design professional or service and trying to design a second home on your own.

Stock Home Plans. Time was when flipping through a catalog of stock home plans was just a way to jump-start your imagination or show your architect a semblance of what you wanted in a vacation home. Today, by sheer volume as well as a commitment to original and creative architectural design and additional services, stock home plans are increasingly the last stop in the process for many homeowners.

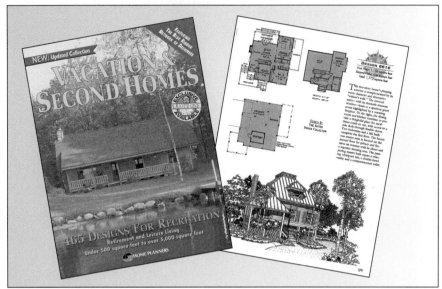

Stock home plan catalogs are often specialized to a particular type of home, including style, size and other design parameters.

Courtesy of Home Planners

From 300-plan catalogs dedicated to vacation and second homes to online access and ordering, home plan services have expanded their design scopes and options, making it easier and less expensive for homeowners to obtain finished construction documents for a second-home project.

> *Stock home plans are increasingly the last stop in the design process for many homeowners.*

For perhaps one percent or less of a $125,000 budget (about $1,200, and often just a few hundred dollars), you can purchase a complete set of plans for a vacation retreat—or at least get about 90 percent of the way there, sans a few homesite- or buyer-specific alterations, which are often made by a local design or building professional you hire.

(In fact, most residential architects and building designers maintain a personal library of their house plans, which they may use to help clients visualize or direct their own projects, offer to alter slightly for cost- and time-conscious clients or sell as a second source of income.)

The growth of stock home plan services, especially for second homes, is a direct reflection of consumers' demand for vacation getaways as well as their disdain for (or lack of appreciation or need of) full-blown architectural design services and fees. It also simplifies the design process by shortening it to a phone call or web search and eliminating any logistical roadblocks, such as distance and priority.

To meet the demand and offer a higher standard of residential design, stock home plan services have brought in or contracted with residential architects and designers to produce new and proprietary plans and/or sell selections from a design pro's existing portfolios of past projects in an increasing variety of catalogs.

Many also have in-house draftspeople able to alter a stock plan slightly to match your precise preferences, such as shifting a wall, expanding a room or changing a peninsula to an island in the kitchen (some plan providers call these "custom" plans, but that label is a bit overstated).

Such services also have evolved their product offerings to include architectural and construction details, worksheets and guidelines for specifications and specialty trade contractors (such as plumbing and electrical) and kits that allow homeowners and their design professionals to alter the basic plans and elevations to suit specific needs or conditions. Some even sell do-it-yourself architectural design software packages.

What You Get. Services vary, but the basic package from a stock home plan seller includes a complete and detailed rendering of the home (called a frontal sheet); technically detailed floor plans and construction documents (blueprints) of the foundation plan; cross-sections (or cutaways) of elevations and key structural elements; and interior and exterior elevation renderings, which show the suggested location of everything from kitchen cabinets and crown moulding to brick accents flanking the entry portico.

Beyond the basic package, home plan services have become savvy to the do-it-yourself crowd with a variety of "extras" that addresses the various design tasks required prior to construction. For instance, a complete materials list may be available for a plan, though mechanical details (plumbing, electrical, HVAC) are left off in deference to local code and other regulatory considerations.

In addition to offering more materials and documentation, stock home plan services also have expanded their ordering options, from mail and fax to online.

Courtesy of Home Planners

(That said, some services sell mechanical guides that spot the suggested locations of plumbing fixtures, pipes and fittings, as well as light switches, wire sizes and other mechanical details that meet nationally recognized building codes.)

Beyond the materials list, some services offer a Specifications Outline, to be completed by the homeowners and their design pro or builder, which spells out the entire scope of construction work, further details the specifications and materials and becomes part of the legal document package with the contract and code-approved blueprints.

These and other materials can be ordered and delivered to your doorstep, giving you the means to either alter them slightly (or simply fill in some blanks with a design professional or builder), or even begin the process of finding and contracting with a builder.

Home Plans Pros and Cons. With ever-expanding portfolios created by in-house designers as well as commissioned architects, stock home plans can likely offer a vacation home that meets your needs and aesthetic tastes. With complete packages of blueprints and other documents, you can be well on your way, if not completely ready, to hiring a builder and starting construction.

Cost is a huge consideration and advantage of stock home plans.

Cost is also a huge consideration and advantage of stock home plans. Where else can you obtain the design work of a residential architect for just a few hundred dollars (or, at most, just over a thousand)? And in the case of stock home plans, "cheap" or inexpensive does not translate into lower quality. In fact, just the opposite is true.

As mentioned earlier, purchasing stock home plans takes much of the hassle out of the design process, shortening it considerably while providing an increasing level of quality and detail. In addition to time saved, there's no travel or meetings, no head butting over a detail and no ego conflict between the designer and builder.

And, if you must hire a design pro to slightly alter the stock plans to accommodate a special need or personal preference, or perhaps a difficult site or climate condition, the bulk of the design work is done and paid for. Hiring someone for a few hours of touch-up work is not only less expensive, but certainly simpler than finding an architect to provide complete design services from the beginning.

The key element missing in the stock home plans option is the value of face-to-face consultation—the hand-holding that is sometimes necessary, but mostly absent in this scenario. An architect or designer helps homeowners match their ideas and priorities for a second home with a two-dimensional floor plan and elevation rendering.

As a page in a home plan book, the plan (and especially the accompanying photo or rendering) may appear to be a perfect fit, but it can be a scary trip from a catalog to construction without a guide. Home plan services help alleviate some fears by offering "review" copies of a plan for as little as $20, providing further detail than what's in the catalog.

Still, unless you have some experience and confidence in your abilities to take the lead in the design of your vacation home (in this case, truly matching your ideas, preferences and homesite conditions with a house style and floor plan), a stock home design may be simply an initial step toward your ultimate goal.

In addition, stock home plans, despite the trend of commissioned designs especially for a given service, are mass-marketed. The home you choose from a catalog may be unique to that plan provider, but it's featured in a book that has been distributed worldwide, where someone else might also choose it. For most folks, such considerations are minor or inconsequential, while others insist on a truly one-of-a-kind plan for their vacation home.

Finding and Buying Home Plans. A keyword search for "home plans" through a popular Internet search engine yielded more than 600 web sites offering stock and custom house plans. Most web sites showcase a service's entire catalog (or series of catalogs) online, and some allow you to narrow your search by specifying square footage and architectural style, among other parameters.

Some folks, however, prefer to curl up on the couch with a good home plans book and find the "perfect plan" among the hundreds contained in a printed catalog. Like an online search, however, home plan catalogs are becoming specialized, either by size (small homes or large luxury houses) and type (vacation homes, waterfront homes), which serve to narrow your focus even in the context of a book.

Home plan books are commonly sold in most bookstores and on newsstands; even libraries may carry a few, though probably not the lat-

Catalogs are continually updated and refreshed to reflect the latest design trends

est editions. With home plan services competing not only among themselves but also with other home design options, catalogs are continually updated and refreshed to reflect the latest design trends and the newest plans from commissioned designers.

Log homes are the trademark of most kit home manufacturers, relying on rustic house designs to inspire vacation- and second-home buyers.

Photo by Trus Joist

You also can find a variety of stock home plan suppliers advertising in the classified section of most home-related magazines, or perhaps featured in a special advertising section or insert showcasing a selection of plans from a new catalog.

The investment in a plans catalog is meager (about $6 - $12) compared to the potential return—a set of plans that meet your needs perfectly for a fraction of the cost to create them from scratch. Plans and accessories can be purchased through the mail (via a form in each book), by calling a toll-free number, or on the Internet if the company has a web site with secure ordering capabilities.

Kit Homes. Like stock home plans, kit homes offer an easier, faster and less expensive method for obtaining complete construction documents, often without having to hire a design professional. In addition to the plans, you also receive the materials to build and finish the house, which are delivered directly to your home site and assembled by a builder (or perhaps you, if you possess the necessary skills and time; see Chapter 6).

Kit home manufacturers are probably best known for log homes and cabins and have gained a particularly strong foothold in the vacation-home market.

Kit home manufacturers are probably best known for designing and selling log homes and cabins and have therefore gained a particularly strong foothold in the vacation- and second-home market for those house styles. Even so, kit (also called "precut" or "factory-built") homes represent less than 5 percent of all new homes built every year, or about 80,000 homes, primarily in rural areas.

As off-the-shelf, mass-produced products, kit homes are a less expensive option for either obtaining plans or building a home, or both. Costs vary due to the type, size and complexity of the home (as well as shipping costs for the building package). The purchase price for the plans alone is comparable to stock house plans, while the materials package—sans the foundation and other site-built features—can be substantially less in cost and assembly time than a conventionally built home.

In many instances, kit homes are sold through local or regional retailers, a fair number of which also can serve as the home's builder or general contractor, or as a technical advisor to another builder. There are two key advantages to this scenario: a local or regional representative will be savvy to the requirements of the area in which you want to build, and is experienced with assembling the system from the manufacturer.

As with stock home plans, kit homes may require the services of a design professional to slightly alter the plans and specifications to fit the conditions of a given home site. Some kit home makers offer such services in-house, but they often lack the ability to conduct high-level engineering for difficult sites; in those cases, it is often necessary—and recommended by the manufacturer—to hire an architect or engineer from that area, or at least one familiar with your chosen location.

Increasingly, kit home manufacturers can refer you to an architect in your area (or chosen location) who has experience with their plans and building systems. Reciprocally, architects may guide their clients to a particular kit home system or supplier, if appropriate to the overall design program and the clients' preferences.

Most kit home manufacturers can refer you to an architect familiar with their materials and system to help manipulate one of their stock plans into your dream vacation home.

Design and rendering courtesy of Kevin McKee Associates

Kit home suppliers also are willing to work with your architect or designer (or builder) to create unique home plans that can be built with their system, which are commonly either a series of interlocking logs or a post-and-beam (timber frame) construction method.

One architect I know, in fact, works almost exclusively with a particular kit home manufacturer to provide vacation and second homes. While the design work is exclusive to his clients, it is done with an eye toward the logs and building system supplied by the manufacturer. Over the years, the architect has even helped refine and improve how the logs go together, while the manufacturer showcases the designer's homes in its sales literature and catalogs.

Kit Home Pros and Cons. As a design option, kit homes are akin to stock home plan services, with similar advantages and limitations. The range of available home styles and sizes is increasing with demand, but kit home designs will always be somewhat limited by the building system used by the manufacturer. Despite efforts to broaden their range, most kit home makers are true to the log and timber-frame-style homes for which they are best known.

Arguably the biggest benefit to a kit home is the time and money saved using a factory-built system to construct your vacation home. Not only are the materials (logs or timbers) most often mass-produced in a factory (and thus less expensive), they arrive at the home site in a precut and labeled package for faster assembly, saving labor costs. (For more on building your vacation home, kit or otherwise, see Chapter 6.)

One potential downside: Though it is certainly possible to purchase only the plans of a vacation cabin from such sources, those plans are often inexorably tied to a particular and proprietary building system, all but requiring that you buy the materials package, as well. While often it is in your best financial interest to do so, some folks resist the idea of buying everything from one supplier.

In fact, like a design-build firm, a kit home manufacturer makes its money on providing a bigger-budget product than simply a set of plans, in this case the complete materials package. Some collect a deposit for design that is then credited to the purchase of the materials package.

If you think a kit home is the best option for your vacation home, seek out suppliers who will ship to your location at no additional charge.

For the most part, therefore, a kit home maker's house plans and design services pique a potential buyer's interest, but aren't relied upon as key revenue sources for the company. The attention paid to you during the design stage, in

Kit home manufacturers offer a wide variety of home styles and sizes, as well as local representatives to guide you through the design and construction processes.

Photo by Northeastern Log Homes

the form of flashy brochures and catalogs, as well as in-house architects and engineers, is most often a means to a more profitable end.

It also may be problematic, cost prohibitive or at least more expensive to ship a kit home package out of the standard range of the factory in which is was manufactured, in some cases adding up to hundreds of dollars extra. If you think a kit home is the best option for your vacation home, seek out suppliers who will ship to your location at no additional charge.

Finding and Buying Kit Homes. As suppliers of both the plans and materials, kit home manufacturers are similar to design-build firms in how they market themselves and make money. Rarely will you find a catalog for a log-home maker on the newsstand, though there are a few magazines exclusively devoted to log and kit homes, with feature articles as well as advertising.

Many kit home makers also follow the lead of stock home plan services by advertising in more general housing-related or lifestyle magazines and/or purchasing extensive inserts to showcase, promote and sell their precut systems.

The Internet has proven to be a solid search tool for kit homes.

The Internet has proven to be a solid search tool for kit homes, and many manufacturers are web-savvy with limited online catalogs, sales information, local rep and contractor referral lists, e-mail feedback and ordering capabilities.

In fact, the same search engine used to identify web sites for "home plans" revealed more than 360 sites under "log homes" (and far fewer for "kit homes," illustrating the industry's primary marketing bent toward cabins and rural home styles), thus providing access to the majority of manufacturers offering such systems.

Kit home manufacturers are anxious to send you a free sales brochure about the company, but many require you to pay—perhaps $20 or more—for a catalog of plans. That said, most of them have created specialized catalogs or may even send you a tailored selection of plans to meet your requested specifications, such as square footage and style.

Commonly, kit home manufacturers are represented by (and will refer you to) local or regional companies that can help facilitate your purchase and perhaps serve as your builder. In addition to being a local contact for a distant company, such folks can give you tours of homes recently built in your area using the manufacturer's system, allowing you to experience the look and feel of a log or timber frame structure and discuss the process with the owners of those homes. The rep may also have a "model" home built for marketing purposes.

As in a design-build scenario, a local rep/builder also can guide you through the "design" process (the selection of an appropriate plan from a catalog) and make slight adjustments to the plan based on your preferences, needs, homesite conditions and overall budget. In addition, a local or regional rep indicates that your area is within the standard shipping range of the manufacturer, which helps keep costs in check.

The purchasing process also is similar to design-build, with an intermediate step (read: a separate contract) for the materials package sandwiched between the design and building phases of the project.

Typically, homeowners make a "deposit" to pay for their chosen plan and in-house design services that may be required prior to construction. If the homeowners decide not to build the plans they've chosen or created, the kit home company keeps the deposit; if the owners go ahead with construction, the deposit is credited to (or taken off) the purchase price of the materials package. The construction contract is usually negotiated separately, as not all local representatives are able to act as the general contractor or builder for the house.

Design-it-Yourself Programs

On the extreme end of design options exist programs and tools to create your own vacation-home design. For folks creative and confident enough to tackle this phase of the process on their own, several software companies have created computer programs to assist that effort.

While these programs rarely yield the technical details required to submit a design for code approval or permit, they do offer a significant amount of flexibility and sophistication in the creation of floor plans and elevations. In addition to helping you properly arrange and size rooms of the house, they provide icons, tools and automated features to specify and show interior and exterior finishes, window shapes and sizes, furniture and other elements.

In addition, some programs will automatically model your design in a three-dimensional perspective (see "Beyond Blueprints," page 103), which helps most homeowners—even those with experience with architectural design or good basic design sense—visualize their vacation home and make adjustments based on a more realistic representation of the plan.

Design (or full-blown CADD) software for architects and engineers is quite expensive, but may run less than $50 for a program geared toward a do-it-yourself home design project. Most require standard PC chip capabilities and memory.

The downside of a design-it-yourself kit or software program is the absence of a true architectural design perspective, the real value of an architect or even a stock home plan or kit home provider. Architecture goes far beyond simply drawing lines on a page or computer screen. Good design incorporates everything from a home's orientation to the sun to a combination or system of building materials and components that optimize its energy use, durability and other performance qualities.

Architecture goes far beyond simply drawing lines on a page or computer screen.

At the very least, gauge your expectations accordingly if you plan to use a home design program. That is, you may be very adept at creating a floor plan and elevations that match your needs and preferences in a vacation home, but neglect other aspects of the design simply because you are not a trained design professional.

Recognize your skills, your role and your limitations. While you certainly must be the driver of your vacation home design to make sure it meets your needs, relying on a design-it-yourself kit or program will be

Your selection of a builder should focus not only on carpentry skills, but also on his or her experience with vacation homes and whether your personalities mesh.

an exercise that more often initiates—rather than completes—the design phase of the project.

Design Tips

No matter which option, or combination of options, you choose for the design of your second home, you should consider certain elements of your vacation retreat differently than you would a primary residence.

Your Wants and Needs worksheet (see Chapter 2) should indicate key differences between what you expect in a vacation home versus a primary home. An architect or other design professional or service will be able to translate those differences on the actual plan and elevations, as will stock home plans and kit homes designed specifically for second and vacation homes.

For instance, while a walk-in closet may be essential in the master bedroom of your main home, such storage is probably unnecessary in a weekend retreat. That said, storage for a golf cart and sets of clubs, snowmobiles, or other recreational toys appropriate to the location of your second home may be a feature not found in your primary residence.

Kitchen design is another area that will probably be different between your two homes. While a nicely styled and fully outfitted kitchen is certainly appropriate for a vacation home, chances are it can be smaller than its counterpart back home. The kitchen may also be part of the living and dining areas, creating a space that encourages conversation and comfort instead of distinctly separate functions.

Similarly, bedrooms can also be smaller and subtler, while outdoor areas, such as decks and patios, will probably play a more prominent role in a second home. Sleeping lofts and porches, game and rec rooms, and a general informality throughout are also common features and traits of a vacation retreat, while a dedicated home office and a formal dining room or parlor are less common, if considered at all.

Of course, you've already set your own course with the preparation you've done prior to the design phase, and your vacation home should reflect your particular lifestyle preferences. Simply, it's important to keep in mind that a second home serves different needs than a primary residence.

> *It's important to keep in mind that a second home serves different needs than a primary residence.*

Toward Construction

With your design work done, it's time to move toward actually building your second home. The transition to the construction side involves getting your design documents in order, defining your role in the building process, and the initial stages of selecting a builder, if one has not already been chosen.

Good versus Bad Documents. A comprehensive set of construction documents is an essential element to a successful construction project. Nothing should be left to chance or question in terms of the design details and specifications. And while changes will likely occur during the building phase, those areas should be red-flagged before the first nail is hammered in.

As much as your building plans are a guidebook to the construction of your house, they also serve to help select your builder. Ambiguity or an incomplete set of plans makes the process of comparing bids and cost estimates almost worthless, as builders struggle to estimate items and circumstances they know will arise but which are lacking on the plans they've been given. The result is often a wide disparity in bid prices and, once construction begins, a recipe for expensive and time-consuming change orders and cost overruns.

For those reasons, it is appropriate to consider hiring a builder or general contractor during the design stage, as with an informal or formalized design-build scenario. The value of a builder's perspective, specifically regarding cost and labor considerations, far outweighs any benefit of the three-bid process (explained in Chapter 6), which takes place at the end of the design phase.

Know Your Role. For many folks, home construction is even more foreign a concept than residential design. Some shy away from the building process, afraid to ask "dumb" questions (hint: there's no such thing) and prefer to simply let the builder take charge. Others manifest their insecurity by hovering over the contractor with a false authority over standards of quality and workmanship or worse, foolishly acting as their own builder or general contractor.

Your role in the building process is important to its success.

Your role in the building process is important to its success, but focuses more on identifying and following through on your responsibilities as the homeowner than pouring concrete or pounding nails. (A book entitled *The Home Building Process* covers this and all other aspects of the construction phases of your vacation-home project. See "For Further Details," page 148)

Simply, you are responsible for finding a builder you can trust, who has the qualifications, skill and experience necessary and relevant to success- fully build your vacation home. You also have a responsibility to under- stand and respect the home building process and your builder, both of which will have ups and downs, exciting and disappointing moments, successes and failures. Chapter 6 will help with that understanding.

Also, just as you have (or will) set a schedule for your builder toward the completion of your second home, you must lead by example by meeting all of your deadlines, as well. A construction schedule can be very sensitive to even the slightest delay, and it's up to you to avoid extending your milestones in the process—and be willing to pay in terms of time and/or extra cost to do so.

Lastly, be candid about your preferences, needs and budget. It makes no practical sense to be coy about what you want and how much you have to spend; if you truly want something, and are willing (and able) to pay for it, expect that it will likely meet those parameters. On the flipside, a constant effort to cut costs or a resistance to exposing your true budget will cause confusion and, most likely, cost overruns.

Finding a Builder. Books and other guides abound about the best way to find and hire a builder or general contractor, but the good ones all come down to one truism: look for a builder you like and can trust.

Look for a builder you like and can trust.

Regardless of what stage you're in when you decide to bring a builder on board, the process is generally the same. Start by gathering the names of builders or contractors in your area and in the location of your vacation home. You can build your list with referrals from your design professional, as well as your family and friends, construction lender or mortgage broker, local building trades association chapter office, building materials retailers who sell primarily to pros and even the phone book or other advertising vehicle—often in that order.

To narrow your list, keep only those builders with experience in vacation or second homes and those who are familiar working with the conditions or features of your chosen home site (such as a steep slope or a high-wind area).

Next, schedule interviews with those on your short list, and come in with specific questions about their current workload, rates and billing procedures and standards for quality and workmanship (and how those are measured or monitored).

Other key areas to explore include methods for supervising subcontractors and suppliers, willingness to work with a design professional or service to refine the plans and troubleshoot problems on the job site, means of communication and financial stability and support.

In addition, ask your builder candidates to share their experiences with vacation- or second-home projects (including photos) and to provide a list of their recent clients. During that phase of the selection process, also notice and note your level of comfort with each candidate, and whether he or she seems to be genuinely concerned and aware of your anxieties and excitement.

Most likely, by the end of your interviews, a clear winner will emerge—one whom you can imagine yourself working with for perhaps several months, and whom you trust to commit to your project in quality, supervision and budget.

Resist the urge (or perhaps the recommendation of your design pro or others) to "bid out" your plans to three candidates as a means to selecting the "best" one. Simply, the three-bid rule reduces builders to mere numbers and

> *Resist the urge to "bid out" your plans to three candidates as a means to selecting the "best" one.*

is rarely an accurate apples-to-apples comparison given varying interpretations of even the most comprehensive set of building plans. Too often, the bidding process breeds resentment and mistrust—the absolute wrong foot to begin the long and sometimes arduous task of building a home.

There's more to a good builder than just someone who can read working drawings and attach a cost to construction. Reward a clearly superior candidate by negotiating an exclusive construction contract.

BUILDING YOUR HOME

Photo courtesy Trus Joist

Expect the construction process to ebb and flow. At times, your vacation home will evolve dramatically, even within a few hours, while progress during other phases will be much slower.

The actual construction of your second home is the culmination of a lot of hard work, and its completion will mark the beginning of a long and enjoyable vacation lifestyle. It's also where reality hits the hardest, when your construction loan kicks in and you watch the physical manifestation of your planning and design efforts unfold.

This chapter will provide insight into the people, paperwork and process of building a home. Within that trilogy, you'll gain a greater appreciation and understanding of your role (and your builder's) and better grasp the details of a complete construction contract that protects both you and your builder.

You'll also receive a primer on the home building process as it typically occurs on the job site, from preparation and structural stages through carpeting and cabinets. By knowing the steps a builder takes to complete a home, the more

By knowing the steps a builder takes to complete a home, the more comfortable and confident you'll be.

A home construction project requires coordination among several trade contractors, suppliers, inspectors and others.

comfortable and confident you'll be to ask prudent questions—and get satisfactory answers.

The People

Gaining a solid understanding of a builder's mindset and motivations—as well as your own role—will help you better communicate with your contractor and go a long way toward a successful project.

The actual construction of a house, regardless of its size, style and location, is basically a simple undertaking for folks who do it for a living. Pouring the foundation, standing up walls, hanging drywall, running electrical wiring—it's nearly second nature for builders, carpenters and a variety of specialty and trade contractors (who are also known as "subs" or subcontractors).

In addition, most builders and contractors are honest, local business people with a particular skill, in this case the ability to build homes. But as adept as most of them are with the tools of their trade, a fair number lack good business and communication skills, and that's the root of most of home building horror stories.

Most commonly, the lack of communication or breakdowns between homeowners and builders occur because of a basic difference in approach to the project, which neither party truly understands nor respects. As the owner of your vacation retreat, for instance, you've spent months—perhaps years—planning for the day when it actually gets built. Your emotional investment is probably equal to or even greater than your financial stake.

That kind of excitement, however, cannot be expected among builders and contractors. Sure, a builder might be thrilled to win the contract for your home, and should be truly committed to meeting your needs, preferences and budget. The best ones, in fact, have a passion for their trade. But the day-to-day progress and process of building a home is routine to a builder, something he does every day, all year.

As much as you may want him to share your excitement, the simple fact is that you'll probably build one vacation home in your life, while he'll build perhaps three or four a year. While you might perceive a problem to be monumental, it's likely he's seen it (and dealt with it) several times before.

Ideally, the builder should respect your excitement and emotional investment in the project, but even so will likely come across a bit more blasé than you'd prefer when difficult issues arise—a relative term given your respective experiences in home building. Understanding that difference is an important key to communicating with your builder.

The two most critical elements of a building project are the schedule and the specifications.

That's why it is vital to select and hire a builder you like personally rather than the one who comes in with the lowest bid (see Chapter 5, page 128). Because it's important for you to be able to talk to your builder, that you share a mutual respect for each other's approach to the project and that he accommodates and encourages communication throughout the construction phase, make those factors a high priority in your selection process.

Delays and Changes
The two most critical elements of a building project are the schedule and the specifications, and it is vital to understand and respect what is

Inclimate weather can delay or even stop a construction project, forcing the builder to adjust the schedule of labor and materials for the project.

Photo courtesy Trus Joist

in your builder's control and what is beyond it. In fact, how your builder prepares for and responds to unforeseen circumstances and ad-hoc changes is one of the best tests of his competence.

For instance, weather delays—especially prone to remote and coastal areas where a vacation home might be built—are generally not your builder's doing. In those cases, however, it is the builder's responsibility to quickly adjust the schedule of other trade contractors and materials deliveries to avoid further delays in the construction schedule.

The construction schedule is, in fact, a very sensitive beast. Each step depends on the completion of the one before it, with trade contractors (such as plumbers and roofers) and materials suppliers (such as lumber yards) committed to a specific time slot based on that premise. When one step is delayed or incomplete, it "dominoes" down the schedule, forcing everyone to adjust to the change.

If the foundation is not completed on time, for instance, delivery of the first load of lumber for the structural frame needs to be pushed back—or left to sit on the driveway. Similarly, a busy plumber may not be able to accommodate a change in the schedule because he's committed to another job, thus forcing further adjustment or a reorganization of the other trades.

The builder's role in maintaining smooth transitions from one step to another depends on his ability to contract with reliable and skilled trade contractors and materials suppliers. As the owner, your role is to adhere to the schedule, as well. If a decision is due (to select the cabinet style or the lighting package, for instance), make sure you're not the one causing a delay. And, if you insist on making a change (called a change order) after the deadline for that decision has passed, be prepared to pay for it in terms of money and lost time.

The Paperwork

The construction contract, along with the set of approved plans and specifications, is the guidebook of the project for both you and your builder. Beyond its legal ramifications and covenants, the contract formally expresses an agreed-upon scope of work and responsibilities (who does what), price, project schedule and materials and specifications. It also specifies payments or "draws," and how those are scheduled, invoiced and paid. The contract may also stipulate certain items not included in the scope of work, so there's no argument about what's to be done.

Commonly, and unfortunately, most construction contracts only skim the surface of details such as change orders, communication and other

Photo courtesy Trus Joist

Communication is a critical element for a successful project, especially between members of the building team.

key considerations beyond the practical and obvious aspects of a building project. And while they often specify an estimated date of completion and a total budget, few contracts are comprehensive enough to cover issues of construction quality and job site conditions that initiate a scheduled payment or meet a homeowner's standards or expectations of quality.

As the homeowner, it is your responsibility to insist on and help create a comprehensive construction contract with your builder (often adapted from a standard contract or agreement), covering every aspect and expectation of the project, starting with the scope of work and including insurance, house rules and legal recourse.

> *It is your responsibility to insist on and help create a comprehensive construction contract with your builder.*

Scope of Work

The scope of work outlines the phases of construction, from securing the building permits (including all applicable fees) to who will supply and install the cabinets and door hardware. Basically, it's a walk-through of the entire construction process that identifies what will happen and by whom (see "The Process," on page 147).

135

The "by whom" aspect of the scope is as critical as the process itself. The contract should identify exactly who, or what subcontractor or supplier, has been hired to deliver and install or assemble the necessary materials for each phase of the project.

Increasingly, subcontractors supply the materials and products they've been hired to install (the electrician's price, for example, often includes the actual wires, switch boxes, outlets, etc., in addition to his labor costs). Even suppliers, such as a lumberyard, will offer "installed sales" for such items as windows and doors, relieving the builder of hiring a separate sub or relying on his own crew to install those products.

Within the scope of work, in fact, a builder's job often resembles a traffic cop among the various trade contractors and materials suppliers. It's an important job that requires as much skill and knowledge as assembling the structural frame. This level of

At times, several trades can be working simultaneously on the exterior and interior of the house.

Photo by James F. Wilson

management, in large part, is why folks who act as their own general contractor often find that job more difficult that they imagined.

For a vacation-home project, however, the typical builder is a small business, operating in often remote or less-populated areas. As such, he may do the bulk of the work himself (with his crew) and only hire out those trade skills he's either not licensed to perform or can accomplish more proficiently and quickly by using a subcontractor. Regardless, the scope of work should identify precisely who will perform each phase of the project.

The scope of work also should identify which phases will require or prompt a building code inspection from the local or nearest authority. Typically, inspections are required—and scheduled by the builder or his on-site superintendent—at certain points in the process. Usually this happens after the foundation is formed ("ready for concrete"); after the home is framed ("rough framing"); once electrical and plumbing systems are installed (or "roughed in"); after the drywall and other wall, roof and floor sheathing are nailed down; once the plumbing and other mechanical work is finished and operating; and upon substantial completion of the house.

Project Schedule

The scope of work may also include, or at least allude to, the project schedule, thus combining what will happen (the scope) with details about when each phase will occur and be completed. The schedule may also be a separate section of, or addendum to, the contract, per-

Photo by Rich Binsacca

Building permits and home inspections are standard practice in urban and suburban housing developments, but the rules may be looser in a more rural setting.

haps shown as a "critical path" or time line, typically with some phases of the project overlapping when appropriate or necessary. (For instance, both the plumber and electrician may be able to work at the same time, in different areas of the house, to rough-in their respective systems.)

In addition, the schedule should include deadlines for making critical decisions, such as the selection of certain products (and who is responsible for making those choices); when products are to be delivered; and when subcontractors are expected to be on the job site—and how long they're expected to take to complete their work.

As mentioned earlier, the initial schedule is an ideal. Generally, a house takes about 100 days (or a hair over three months) to complete. However, changes and delays can occur during the project that cause the builder (with your approval or at least knowledge) to adjust and often lengthen the schedule. Whether there's been a delay or adjustment, the schedule specified in the contract should be discussed between you and your builder at least on a weekly basis, and certainly when ad-hoc changes need to be made.

Photo courtesy Trus Joist

A properly designed home will allow the optimum use of materials to help reduce labor and materials costs.

Payment Schedule and Procedure

Every contract specifies the overall or total price of the project, usually the amount of your construction loan and agreed budget. But as outlined in Chapter 3, the schedule and procedure for initiating a draw (a release of funds) from your loan or other payment source can be complex—and thus require more specific details in the contract.

Commonly, the payment schedule will specify a down payment—typically about ten percent—to "mobilize" the builder and provide him with some operating cash to establish and prepare the job site and order the first load of materials and equipment.

After that initial step, the payment schedule typically follows either the start of, or the approved completion of, certain phases of the project, as defined in the scope of work. The contract also should specify the billing procedure (via vouchers, statements and other paperwork to back up the amount) and even what day of the week it will be paid and how, either by a personal check, bank voucher or direct deposit into the builder's account. The latter is a more common or agreeable method given the likely distance between your builder (and vacation home) and where you and your primary residence are located.

Commonly, draws are made after the foundation is poured, once the rough frame is assembled, upon completion of rough mechanicals (plumbing, electrical, waste disposal and heating/cooling), after sheathing and drywall is hung and nailed, and upon the installation of the basic finishes, such as the cabinets and carpeting.

Ideally, draws are used to pay for the labor and materials costs of the phase just completed. This is a stipulation that should be obvious and agreed to in the contract, and backed up by the collection of lien releas-

Photo courtesy Trus Joist

Framing can be a fascinating stage of the process to watch, as walls are built, erected and fastened quickly to form the basic structure and shape of the house.

es or waivers (usually by the builder) proving that subs and suppliers have been paid for work done on your house.

Without that stipulation, you run the risk of the builder using your money to pay for bills on another (often previous) project. This leaves the subs and suppliers working on your vacation retreat with no other recourse than to demand payment directly from you—even though you've already paid your builder for that purpose.

That's why so many construction lenders prefer to pay subs and suppliers on a voucher system or through a third party (see Chapter 3, page 68), a condition any good builder will agree to without hesitation. In fact, relieving a builder of that accounting chore will allow him to focus on the work rather than the books.

The final draw is tied to the completion of the house and the issuance of a Certificate of Occupancy (or CO) by the building code authority. The last payment is also about ten percent of the overall budget, and represents the gross profit most builders make on a house contract.

Specifications
On the plans you'll see a sheet, or perhaps a box on several sheets, list-

The specifications should be listed in the contract, perhaps in even greater detail than on the construction drawings.

ing the various products to be used in the construction and completion of the house. Called the specifications, these lists are vital to the builder, subcontractors, suppliers, building code inspectors and plan checkers. But having them on the plans is not enough.

In addition, the specifications should be listed in the contract, perhaps in even greater detail than on the construction drawings. Each product, in fact, should be referenced by its brand name, model number, color, size or dimension, count (i.e., number of total pieces or amount, such as for floor tile), as well as where it is to be installed in the house, plus applicable warranties and service agreements and perhaps the product's supplier. Each kitchen cabinet, each bathroom faucet and towel bar, each wall outlet and dimmer switch—right down to the light bulbs.

Why such detail? Again, the purpose of the plans and contract is to protect you and your builder from confusion and miscalculation, as well as provide the best guide possible for the entire project. A detailed list of specifications in the contract removes all mystery and allows you and the builder to check a materials delivery against that list.

The specifications also help subcontractors estimate the cost of their work and that of the materials and products they're often contracted to supply. They'll also perhaps be able to suggest alternatives if a product is hard to find, more expensive than you or your design-build team anticipated or one that can be replaced by another product that performs better than the original specification.

Change Orders

Despite all the detail and planning, changes will occur during the construction of your vacation home. Whether initiated by you or suggested by your builder or a subcontractor, change orders should require a formal policy and procedure that is stated in the contract.

Change orders should be stated as a formal policy and procedure in the contract.

Commonly, a change order policy involves a written and signed form that specifies the scope of the change, its cost, when and how it will be paid for and its impact (if any) on the schedule, overall budget and estimated date of completion.

It may seem like an awful lot of work to simply swap the cabinet finish from maple to pine, but a change order policy and procedure assures accountability and knowledge of the change among everyone involved. In fact, it may prompt you to rethink an alteration in the plans or specifications if the cost and/or time to make the change are too great. It also allows you to keep tabs on your builder and subcontractors should you see an unapproved alteration made on the job site.

A change order policy is especially important with a vacation-home project, mostly because you're probably not going to be on the job site, or even in communication with your builder, on a daily basis given the proximity of the project to your primary residence. More likely, you'll make periodic or scheduled visits at key stages (see "Communication," on page 144). When you get there, you may see things that don't appear to mesh with how you interpreted the plans and specs. A change order policy should remove any mystery and provide some level of comfort as the project progresses.

Photo courtesy Trus Joist

Completion of the structural frame represents a significant milestone in the home construction process, typically triggering a payment to the contractor.

Lien Releases and Waivers

In addition to clearly stating that the builder is to use your funds to pay the subs and suppliers to your vacation home project, the contract should stipulate a provision for the collection of lien releases and waivers—specifically, who will collect them and when such waivers are required to be on record and available for review by the lender and you.

Lien releases or waivers are legal documents that remove any liability for

There should be no more work to be done, nor money to be paid, for a specified scope of work once a subcontractor or supplier issues a lien release.

payment to a subcontractor, supplier or other contracted vendor specific to a phase or section of work that has been completed to everyone's satisfaction. There should be no more work to be done, nor money to be paid, for a specified scope of work once a subcontractor or supplier issues a lien release.

For instance, the plumber may be contracted to perform two stages of work—the rough-in or installation of the pipes and later, the installation of the various plumbing fixtures and fittings (called the "finish"). Once the rough-in has been completed and approved, and the plumber has been paid for that stage of his contract, the builder should collect a lien release to that effect. Another waiver will be collected once the finish work is done, approved and paid for. Or, the plumber may issue a single lien release at the completion of all the work.

Lien releases and waivers are commonly required when a third-party payment system is in place (see Chapter 3, page 68), providing another layer of assurance for the lender and you that draws are being used to pay for your project and that the budget or loan amount is on course. But even if you're paying for your vacation retreat out of your own pocket, a stated policy for lien releases and waivers is an essential element of the construction contract.

Warranties

In addition to any product or system warranties listed with the specifications (see above), the contract should stipulate other provisions for service work related to the home's performance, products and systems.

Specifically, the contract should specify a warranty program or provision for the overall structural quality and performance of the house. Most building-industry warranty programs—structured similarly to liability insurance and taken out in the builder's name—cover all defects related to the home's construction for about a year or two, and structural problems (foundation, frame) for perhaps ten or more years.

Commonly, the builder pays a premium into an independent warranty program to cover any claims, and should require his subcontractors (in their contracts) to also carry some sort of warranty or other insurance against defects within their specific scopes of work. Some builders (and subs) have taken to self-insurance programs. If that's the case, just make sure it's adequately funded and comparable in its coverage terms to a standard warranty program.

In addition to a structural and performance warranty on your vacation home, the contract should define the terms, conditions and claims procedures of each product or service warranty offered by product manufacturers, suppliers, subcontractors and the builder—such as the extent of the policy and who will administer it. For instance, a warranty from an appliance manufacturer may state that service work can be done by an authorized local dealer, or may require the product be repackaged and returned for any covered service work.

Service calls, or "call-backs," are common with new homes as products and systems require ad-hoc adjustment to reach optimum performance. With a vacation house, however, a policy and procedure for call-backs is a little tougher to administer, given that you'll only occasionally live in your second home and may miss a window of opportunity to require additional work.

Stipulate in the contract an agreed-upon schedule for call-backs or service work within the first year of the home's completion.

In that case, it is perhaps better to stipulate in the contract an agreed-upon schedule for call-backs or service work within the first year of the home's completion—perhaps tied to seasonal or climate changes that would prompt the use of certain products or systems, such as the furnace.

And because you're an occasional or seasonal resident in your chosen location, it is even more critical that the contract list the trade contractors (ideally, those that worked on your house) and/or service agencies or companies in that location that can respond to a problem, whether it's covered under warranty or not ... and even whether you're in the house or not.

In addition to the names and phone numbers of any local service outlets or contractors, the service and warranty section of the contract

Photo courtesy Trus Joist

During construction, scheduled and ad-hoc meetings among the contractor, architect, trades and homeowner can help keep the project on schedule and help alleviate any misunderstandings about the process or progress.

should also specify the expected response time and cost (often per hour) for those folks, as well as your builder, once a call is made.

Communication

If a construction contract was to be structured by areas of importance, provisions for communication should arguably top the list. You can have the greatest plans, the most comprehensive payment provisions, policies and procedures for every conceivable aspect of the project, but it will all go for naught without effective communication.

Communication during the construction of a vacation home is vital to maintain trust and confidence between you and your builder.

As mentioned earlier, builders and homeowners approach a vacation-home project quite differently, which often causes a breakdown in communication. Builders also talk a very different and industry-specific language, using terms that most homeowners find unfamiliar and are afraid to clarify. In the heat of a project, especially one you cannot keep an eye on every day, anxiety often overcomes any contractual assurances.

Even more so than building a new primary residence, communication during the construction of a vacation home is vital to maintain trust and confidence between you and your builder. As you work through the construction schedule, keep a calendar handy and list in the contract when you plan to visit the job site.

With that, state the reason for the visit, such as to take a framing walk-through, see the roof trusses installed or be on hand when the kitchen cabinets arrive. It will also help your builder to know the time of day you plan to arrive and how long you plan to stay so he can make time for your visit and schedule deliveries and contractors accordingly.

If you feel the need to visit the site more often, that's fine—but be sure you have an agenda, thus giving you and your builder at least a starting point of discussion when you arrive and an agreed level of expectation for what's to be completed or in progress. If you want the electrician to join you on the framing walk-through (so you can locate, or "spot," the various outlets to your liking), make sure that's stated in this section of the contract.

Because your site visits will likely be a week or more apart, also specify other methods of regular communication, such as by phone, e-mail and fax (with all the appropriate numbers and addresses listed, of course). For instance, you may want your builder to call you at the end of each workweek and perhaps provide a simple progress report via fax or e-mail for your review and discussion. Such communication also can serve as a reminder of upcoming scheduled payments or code inspections or to facilitate change orders.

As with warranty work and site visits, stipulate an agreed response time to phone calls and e-mails, or perhaps even a time you'll call, so that your builder can set aside time to focus on the conversation. A callback within a few hours is reasonable, as is a next-day reply to an e-mail.

Here or There, Part 2

As discussed in Chapter 5, you'll need to determine whether to hire a builder from the location of your primary residence or closer to the area of your vacation home. For the most part, it's probably smarter to find a builder in your vacation-home location, primarily because of his or her familiarity with the local codes, labor force, materials suppliers and construction methods.

Choosing that option, however, distances you from the project and may cause some anxiety and stress as you wonder how the project is progressing. In addition to stipulating a clear plan for regular communication and visits to the job site, you may also want to consider extending the contract of your design professional (especially if he or she also works in the area of your vacation home) to act as a liaison and supervisor on your behalf during construction.

Or, if your design pro is located nearer your primary residence and the cost of his or her time is prohibitive (or if you used stock home plans or bought a kit home without the services of a design professional), consider hiring a reputable liaison, perhaps a local lender, home inspector or mortgage broker, to at least provide a third-party perspective to the project.

Pre-construction Conference

Part of the overall communications plan is a meeting among the key players on the project, including yourself, the builder and/or his site superintendent (if there is one), the design professional, and perhaps a few key subcontractors.

The overriding purpose of the conference, typically held at the builder or architect's office, is to put faces with names and establish the basic roles and responsibilities of those involved. More specifically, the agenda should include scrutinizing the construction schedule, product specifications and scope of work, as well as filling in any blanks and fleshing out any concerns about any aspect of the contract or other conditions.

Even though you are ultimately responsible for the success of the project, it's probably best to let your builder (or perhaps design pro, depending on his stated role) run the pre-construction meeting. Beforehand, discuss your primary areas of concern and gain a solid understanding of what your builder or architect wants to accomplish at the meeting. Once it starts, be willing to ask questions and generally participate in the discussion.

Depending on the flow of the work and your satisfaction with its progress, you may consider a similar meeting at a critical stage of the project, perhaps after the rough framing is completed. At that point, a new set of subcontractors will begin to invade the job site, and it might serve you and your builder well to gather them up and follow a similar agenda to the initial meeting, as well as work out any kinks you've discovered since.

Legal Recourse

No one wants to think about having to take legal action against their builder or a subcontractor or supplier to your vacation-home project, but it is necessary to stipulate in the contract an agreed legal path for handling disputes and disagreements beyond your other communication methods.

Increasingly, builders and homeowners are agreeing to mediation and arbitration as alternative means of resolving legal disputes, thus avoiding more expensive lawsuits and trials. Mediation and arbitration services are available in most areas, and some are focused specifically on construction issues. In fact, some building trade organizations may have in-house services, or references to nearby agencies, to get you started.

Anything that even remotely relates to your vacation-home project should be stated somewhere in the construction contract.

Other Conditions

Suffice to say that anything—and I mean anything—that even remotely relates to your vacation-home project should be stated somewhere in the construction contract. For instance:

- **Penalties and Incentives.** Reward (or punish) your builder for adherence to the budget, schedule and standards you've both established; a similar clause might tie a penalty (to you) for late payment, or perhaps a discount for bills paid early.

- **Job Site Conditions.** Got a fetish for neatness, even on a construction site? In fact, a clean and well-kept job site is a sign of a professional and well-organized builder. In addition, specify where and how materials and equipment will be stored and protected on the job site, as well as provisions and procedures for waste removal, signage, noise and emergency or medical conditions.

• **Special Requests.** Make sure the builder knows you want to use that old claw-foot tub in your basement for the master bathroom in your vacation retreat—and who is responsible for refurbishing it and hauling it up to the project. A special request may also state your preferences for where vehicles, dumpsters and porta-johns are parked or placed on the site.

• **Building Code Compliance and Recourse.** It does NOT go without saying that the plans and specifications should meet all applicable building codes and other regulatory conditions, such as zoning laws and hazardous waste removal. Make sure they do in the contract, and specify who and how any violations will be handled.

The Process

Along with understanding the people working on your vacation-home project and the paperwork involved, it pays to have a bit of insight into the home building process. You may already have recognized that construction has its own language, but it also has its own pace that deserves your respect, or at least recognition.

Specifications and other details should be used to dictate and evaluate the level of precision and quality of workmanship during construction.

Photo by James F. Wilson

While rarely exactly the same for every builder, the home building process typically follows a similar track, from the initial preparation of the homesite through the foundation, structural frame, installation of mechanical systems and prefinishes, and the final stages of exterior and interior finishes and fixtures.

You are not expected to become an instant expert on home building. However, a crash course will help ease some anxieties along the way.

In your role as the owner, you are not expected to become an instant expert on home building. However, a crash course will help ease some anxieties along the way. (There's also a helpful book that goes into much greater depth on this topic; see "For Further Details," below.)

With that knowledge base, you'll also be able to ask more pointed and intelligent questions, and be able to demand and properly interpret more direct answers from your builder.

For Further Details

Want to know why it seems to take forever to finish a house, or why the plumbing contractor always needs to come back twice to finish his work? If you feel the need to bone up on every detail related to residential construction, curl up with *The Home Building Process*, also by this author. The book takes a step-by-step approach to how a home is built, and offers insight into the options available, the motivations and decision-making processes of builders and contractors, and the language of the construction industry. There's also a helpful "running clock" that follows each step and the entire process. The book, published in 2000, is available at most online and retail booksellers nationwide, or through Home Planners, in Tucson, Arizona (see "Resources and Bibliography," page 178).

Site Preparation

The conditions of your homesite, including its soil content, the location of the water table and frost line, and the site's natural slope or grade, combine to determine the finished house—most especially the type of foundation and even the location and size of the windows and the choice of exterior finish.

Preparing the homesite for construction includes several steps, initiated by a soils test and a survey of the parcel (identified by stakes set into the

Excavation represents the first stage of actual construction, when the footings, foundation and utility trenches are dug.

ground), which establish the basic conditions and parameters of the home's location on the site.

Once confirmed and approved (if necessary, by the local building code authority), the survey stakes are replaced by a series of batter boards and taut string lines used to better define the shape and dimensions of the home's foundation per the construction documents or "prints." The batter boards also guide the excavator for the trenches that outline the construction of the foundation. The taut lines, meanwhile, can be used to estimate the eventual height of the foundation walls.

The excavation stage is next. Typically, the excavator will remove a foot-deep layer of topsoil around the outline of the foundation, to be used later as backfill and to help shape or regrade the homesite for optimum drainage. Using heavy equipment, such as a backhoe, the excavator also gouges out the foundation trenches and/or footings, the depth and size of which are determined by the soil conditions and the type of foundation to be constructed.

In addition to trenches for the foundation and footings, the excavator also will dig canals for the installation of the underground pipes and conduits of the main utilities coming from the curb (or nearest hub) to

Utilities, such as natural gas, electric and/or water, are "stubbed up" next to the house and connected at a later stage of construction.

Photo by Rich Binsacca

the house. These will be capped and "stubbed up" above grade near the eventual location of the service panel and meters for connection later.

The Foundation

Your vacation home will likely have one of three types of foundations—slab-on-grade, crawlspace or full basement—depending on the conditions of your homesite as well as local building codes, typical construction practices and materials availability.

A slab-on-grade foundation is simply a flat section of concrete (with footings, explained below), resting directly on the excavated soil, which serves as the first-floor platform of the house. A crawlspace foundation is set a few feet above the excavated soil (or grade), creating a cavity for the installation of and access to various utilities. It also allows the construction of a wood-framed floor (or first platform) spanning the perimeter walls of the foundation.

Finally, a full basement foundation is dug deep into the homesite (at least eight feet below grade), with a slab at the base and walls extending to or just above the excavation. Like a crawlspace, a basement allows for the construction of a wood-framed first-floor platform at grade, but also creates a usable below-grade area for living space, storage or other uses.

Despite their differences, each of these foundation types requires formwork, footings and anchors. Formwork (or forms) is simply the mold into which concrete and reinforcing steel are placed and set, and then stripped away and reused elsewhere. The footings, set into undisturbed soil deeper than the eventual floor or foundation slab (as well as below the frost line and above the water table), anchor the foundation to the homesite and carry and distribute the weight (or load) of the house, as well as reduce movement or settling of the structure. Footings also are used for peripheral elements, such as chimneys, partitions and other localized loads. Anchors are commonly steel bolts embedded in the foundation to tie the structural frame—most often wood—to the concrete.

Footings are excavated, reinforced with steel bars (called rebar) and poured with concrete first, or perhaps in tandem with a foundation or basement slab to create a monolithic structure.

The walls of a crawl-space or full basement are formed next, the latter with preformed panels measuring about the size of a sheet of plywood (4 x 8 feet) and set four inch-

Photo by James F. Wilson

Once the wall forms for a basement or above-grade wall are set in place, the contractor and his crew work quickly to pour and properly place the concrete.

es apart, creating a deep canal for rebar and concrete. In some cases, formwork will not be necessary, such as if the builder chooses to excavate the mold out of the site (typically reserved, if at all, for slab-on-grade jobs), or use concrete blocks, or CMUs, to build the basement or foundation walls.

Once the concrete is set (or curing) the formwork is stripped away, leaving bare concrete on both interior and exterior faces of the wall. For full basements designed for living space, the process may include the application of a waterproofing system—typically a membrane and insulation panels—to maintain dry conditions and guard against hydrostatic pressure below grade. If left unprotected, the backfilled walls of a full basement may give way to water pressure and begin to leak or at least show signs of moisture infiltration.

Lastly, every basement type requires an anchoring system to secure the structural frame to the foundation. Typically, a series of anchor bolts (or J-bolts, so-called because of their shape) are embedded into the wet concrete immediately after it is poured. The bolts are set about eight inches apart and their threaded ends extended at least three inches above the top of the foundation walls or slab to bolt down a 1½-inch-thick piece of lumber called a sill plate—the first component of the structural frame.

Photo courtesy HGTV

The first and subsequent floor frame structures create a flat and secure platform for construction of the walls.

Before the excavator returns to backfill the trenches around the foundation walls and groom the grade for proper drainage, your plans may call for the installation of a perimeter drainage system—a series of perforated plastic pipes that will carry water away from the foundation. In essence, the drainage system is an underground gutter system.

Once installed, the drainage system is protected by a layer of washed pea gravel and then backfilled with the topsoil excavated earlier in the process. The excavator fills the trenches and smoothes the grade to within about eight inches of the top of the foundation wall. Leaving some of the wall exposed and clear of the fill keeps ground water and moisture from edging up to the wood frame components of the house—a much more permeable and vulnerable material than concrete.

The Structural Frame

More than any other phase of home construction, the building of the structural frame is the most dramatic. Within a few weeks, your vacation home rises from a set of two-dimensional, quarter-inch-scale plans to a full-scale, three-dimensional model.

In addition to being a structural entity, similar to your own skeletal system, the frame design and construction also determine in some measure the overall performance of your second home, from its insulating value and resistance to climate conditions to whether the floor squeaks and the doors and windows operate properly.

Most homes, vacation or not, are built using a method called platform framing, in which each level of the house, from the foundation up, is a separate—yet also interconnected—structure built on a platform.

Photo courtesy Trus Joist

To help ensure "squeak-free" floors, high-quality framing contractors secure the plywood sub-floor panels to the floor joists with glue, then screw them in place.

For homes with a crawlspace or full basement foundation, the first-floor platform is created by a series of joists that span from one wall to another, sometimes supported by posts at critical points along that span. The joists, typically 2x10s, 2x12s or engineered I-joists of comparable dimension, are laid out across the foundation. A rim (or perimeter) joist is nailed to the exposed ends of the joists along the foundation perimeter, enclosing the platform frame and stabilizing the joists.

Once the joists are in place, the builder or framing subcontractor will install and secure the sheathing panels, often sheets of plywood or oriented strand board (OSB) nailed or screwed (and sometimes also glued) to the tops of the joists, resulting in a platform upon which the walls will be constructed.

Walls and Roof

A basic residential wall section consists of a horizontal plate at the bottom, vertical studs and another horizontal plate at the top. With the vertical studs are openings for doors and windows, many featuring a deeper section of wood spanning the top of the opening called a header. The top plate may be doubled to carry additional weight from above (such as a second-floor platform and frame, as well as the roof), or to achieve a desired ceiling height.

The most common wall-framing material is the 2x4 wood stud, which actually measures 1.75 inches by 3.5 inches and stands a bit less than eight feet high (with the sill and top plate, a framed wall will measure eight feet). The spaces (or cavities) between the studs accommodate the placement of insulation, wiring, plumbing and other components.

Once all of the exterior walls are constructed on the first-floor platform, either another platform and wall system are constructed for the second-floor living space, or the roof trusses are built and installed. If your vacation home has a second story or level, the same steps apply as to the first platform frame, with the top plates of the first-floor walls doubling as the bottom plates for the second-floor joists, and so on.

If your second home is a single-level structure, however, the exterior walls (and sometimes a few interior walls) will support the weight of the roof. The roof structure is either a series of factory-built trusses (used mostly for simple roof designs) or will be "stick-built" on the job site by the framing subcontractor or builder's crew of workers.

On simple roof designs, a series of plated trusses, fabricated in a factory and trucked to the job site, allows the roof structure to be built quickly and easily.

In rural and even resort areas, stick-framing a roof is more common than factory-built trusses, typically because a reliable, local source of such trusses is unavailable, unreliable or cost-prohibitive in terms of

Photo courtesy Jason Munroe/Idaho Truss

The application of exterior wall sheathing sets the stage for the application of exterior finishes and other products, including siding, windows and trim.

shipping expense. Regardless of the roof framing system, though, the structure itself will likely feature dormers, skylights, chimneys, vent pipes and other intrusions.

The final stage of rough framing is the sheathing, both of the walls and roof (or any exposed framing), with sheets of plywood or OSB applied to the outside, or exterior, side of the framing. The corners of the house frame, in fact, may already have been sheathed to provide lateral support for the exterior walls while interior walls and the roof structure were being built.

Rough Mechanicals

Once the entire house is sheathed (or "buttoned up," industry lingo for this stage in the process), the rough (or first) stage of the mechanical

Inside, the installation of the "rough" mechanicals, such as heating and cooling ducts, electrical wiring and plumbing, must be completed and inspected before drywall can be applied.

Photo courtesy of Ideal Homes

systems involves the installation of the behind-the-wall interworkings, with a second (or finish) stage occurring later in the process.

The three main mechanical systems of a home are electrical, plumbing (including natural gas, if appropriate) and heating, ventilation and air conditioning (commonly referred to as HVAC). Each requires its own subcontractor and crew of workers to install. Additional services, such as cable television, in-home security, telephone and data wiring and fire sprinkler systems are also installed at this time. Usually, only a few additional contractors are required for these secondary networks, as the same subcontractor often handles systems such as security and telephone/data.

There is no prescribed order for the installation of the mechanical rough-ins, though a good builder will determine the order—and any special requirements—as part of creating the construction schedule. The result, however, is a maze of pipes, wires and metal ducts (or conduits for the HVAC), all of which are brought to a point ready to finish, such as a light switch, kitchen faucet and vent registers. In fact, the systems remain in their unfinished state until the drywall and so-called "prefinishes," as well as most of the interior finishes, are applied, at which time the builder recalls the various mechanical subcontractors to complete their work.

"Prefinishes" serve as transitions between the rough stages of construction and the finishes and details of a completed house.

Prefinishes

In fact, there is no such term as "prefinishes" in housing lingo, but the word does serve the purpose of combing such components as insula-

Insulation is used primarily to slow the rate of thermal transfer through the exterior walls, but can also be applied to help deaden noise inside the home.

Photo by James F. Wilson

tion, windows and doors and drywall into one general stage of the construction process.

These and associated steps serve as transitions between the rough stages of construction and the finishes and details of a completed house. Drywall or gypsum panels, for instance, cover and protect the rough framing and mechanical systems, and also act as a substrate for finishes such as paint, wallpaper and ceramic tile.

In addition, all of the "prefinish" components create what is commonly referred to as the home's thermal envelope, or the protection of the inte-

Prebuilt windows (and doors) make for fast and simple installation, helping speed the construction process and reduce labor costs.

Photo courtesy CertainTeed

rior, livable space from outside elements. Insulation, for example, reduces the amount of heat that flows through the walls.

In typical order of installation, the prefinish stage consists of insulation of various types (often applied in combination to create a "tight" house that restricts heat transfer and airflow through the structure); windows and doors (which have thermal value and also provide ventilation and access to the house); and drywall, with its myriad layers that create a smooth, flat surface for finishes (see below).

> *The exterior and interior finishes often take the longest to complete of any stage in the process.*

Finishes

The exterior wall sheathing and "prefinishes" stages create an enclosed thermal envelope and signal the start of the next phase of construction: applying the exterior and interior finishing touches to your vacation home. These stages—often done in tandem to save time—consist of an impressive number of components and require precise skill for proper installation and application. Therefore, the exterior and interior finishes often take the longest to complete of any stage in the process, requiring patience on your part as you anticipate moving into and enjoying your second home.

Exterior finishes typically include the roofing, siding, trim, lighting and gutters attached to the house. The application of other features and products, such as pathways, patios, fences, site drainage and various landscaping, are often dictated by the contract, and may require a separate agreement (and contractor) to complete.

Even moreso than exterior finishes, the interior of your home is comprised of hundreds of finishing components, materials and products. A glance into the kitchen of your primary residence (or at the list of specifications for your vacation home's kitchen), in fact, offers a microcosm of this stage of the process, from floor, wall and ceiling finishes and treatments to lighting, plumbing, HVAC, electrical, storage (in the form

Installation of the exterior trim can be a slow phase of the process, but the results will likely be dramatic.

Photo courtesy Style-Solutions

Properly constructed floors and walls
make installation of the kitchen and bathroom cabinets and other finishes faster
and easier.

Photo by James F. Wilson

of cabinets), and other surfaces. It's a telling indication of the coordination, time and extent of work required to finish a home for occupancy.

Regardless of the style and expense of the products used, finishing the
interior of your vacation home primarily is an amalgam of little tasks:
attaching electrical faceplates, vent registers and towel racks, priming
and painting walls and trim, hanging wallpaper and cabinets, laying
floor finishes, setting tile and installing faucets, toilets and tubs.

To accomplish those tasks, the various subcontractors and other
installers must be coordinated depending on their availability and in a
logical sequence, a schedule that is rarely smooth or without some delay
or downtime between crews of workers.

Ready for Occupancy?

In the housing industry, the installation of carpeting is generally considered to be the sign of a finished house or "significant completion," trig-

gering a final inspection (if required) and the issuance of a Certificate of Occupancy (or CO), assuming everything is in good order.

In addition, there are some other administrative loose ends to tie up, all of which you should have been made aware of by your builder prior to construction, if not in the contract itself (covered in Chapter 7). From a walk-through to punch-list items, the last few days of construction can be tedious. The result, however, is a finished vacation home—the culmination of your dreams, plans, preparation and hard work.

Paint is one of the final—and often longest—phases of construction, requiring painstaking detail and care.

YOUR RETREAT IS READY

The completion of your vacation home retreat is truly a dream come true.

It would be impossible to adequately express how relieved and over-joyed you'll feel when your vacation home is finished. Regardless of the experience, but especially if you followed the steps and advice in this book, you will feel a tremendous sense of accomplishment and, hopefully, satisfaction.

The "move-in" process, however, is probably going to be a bit different than it was with your primary residence. It may actually take you a few months of day and weekend trips to adequately furnish and otherwise ready your second home for an actual vacation experience. You may want to order and oversee the delivery of furniture, among other finish-

Often, the move-in process to a vacation home takes longer than a primary residence, perhaps spanning several weeks or months before the house is completely outfitted.

es and fixtures (like that claw-foot tub from the basement of your primary home).

In addition, there are a few other items on your personal punch list before you begin enjoying your vacation getaway, including a review of warranty and service work policies and procedures, some training on the operation of various systems in the house and various maintenance and care-taking considerations.

You'll also make a final payment to the builder and gather up any lingering lien releases for the file, kept either by you or your lender. Depending on your financial circumstances, you'll want to convert your construction loan to a permanent second-home mortgage (discussed in Chapter 3).

Your builder also has some remaining responsibilities: scheduling a final inspection (and making sure the house passes); securing a Certificate of Occupancy (CO) by the local building authority; crossing off every one of his punch list items; and generally tidying up the job site and removing all of his gear and equipment.

Warranty Work

As mentioned in Chapter 6, in the context of the construction contract, it should be very clear to you what steps to take if a product, system or material fails to meet your expectations after move-in. Whether it's a defect, poor performance, or simply a break-down in operation, every component of your house should be tied to a service procedure.

By law, in fact, often at the state level, builders are held accountable for the condition and code compliance of their homes after the sale. This type of warranty is "implied," which means that it need not be written down or even signed by you or the builder to be enforced.

Often, however, builders will formalize the process by presenting an "expressed" warranty, a written document outlining the terms and responsibilities for maintaining the house and addressing any structural or other needs within a stated amount of time. While such a warranty is best (and typically) spelled out in the contract, revisit that section of the document before you take legal possession of the house.

Photo courtesy Town & Country Cedar Homes

Furnishing and finishing a second home should reflect how you plan to enjoy your vacation retreat.

Make sure you are comfortable and confident that the house is completed to your satisfaction before closing escrow and taking legal ownership of your second home.

Photo courtesy of Hearthstone Homes

Limited warranties that cover major structural defects for perhaps ten or more years (and all components for a year or two) are different from your homeowner's insurance policy and the separate warranty policies and paperwork you'll receive covering parts and labor on specific products. Some subcontractors will offer limited warranties for their work, as well, though usually only at the request or requirement of the builder.

These and other warranties exist for your protection. Most go unused, whether because the products and systems perform as promised or because homeowners resist asking for warranty service when it is needed or appropriate. Resist that reluctance by insisting that things work properly and consistently, and do your part to make sure

If the house meets code and your expectations, you need to let your builder off the hook and take responsibility for its maintenance.

you're not contributing to any flaws or failure from neglect or improper use and care.

Even the best builders, however, need eventually and decidedly to move on from your project, in essence distancing themselves legally from the care and condition of your vacation home after you move in. If the house meets code and your expectations, you need to let your builder off the hook and take responsibility for its maintenance.

Occupational Training

That's a play on words, but the point is to make sure your builder (and perhaps the appropriate subcontractors) walk through the house with you to explain and demonstrate the various products and systems in the home. Even more important than with your primary residence (simply because you won't be using the house's systems every day), a walkthrough and demo will allow you to ask questions and test the operation of each system under the guidance of its installer. Be prepared to take notes, or at least recognize the instruction manuals and put them in a safe but memorable place.

Photo courtesy of Town & Country Cedar Homes

Part of your responsibility as an owner is to understand how various elements and systems of the house operate, as well as how to maintain them over time.

Another walk-through should be conducted with your builder. Unlike the demo version, this one takes place after the final inspection but before you take legal possession of the house. Its purpose is to identify and document remaining items to be installed or repaired and set a schedule for that work. It is, in most cases, your final opportunity to ask questions and get what you want from your builder.

Punch list items include things such as paint touch-ups, loose tiles, and missing or broken finishes—a cracked faceplate or busted light bulb—mostly minor stuff that requires an hour or

Flaws in workmanship often can be remedied and therefore should be added to the punch list.

167

two of a general carpenter's time to repair or replace. Your contractor may also have a list from an internal walk-through he conducted earlier. In addition, flaws in workmanship, while often a subjective judgment, often can be remedied and therefore should be added to the punch list.

It is important to realize that you have more leverage with a builder before close of escrow than after that date.

The date to complete all of the punch-list items might be before or after close of escrow or move-in, depending on when those events occur and your comfort level. However, it is important to realize that you have more leverage with a builder before close of escrow than after that date, when you are the legal owner of the home.

At the walk-through, the builder may also present you with a homeowner's handbook containing information and instructions about the products and systems in your home, warranty details and service call-back procedures. The handbook also may include some courtesy items, such as a certificate from the painting contractor to return for touch-ups after you move in (as you're bound to scrape a few walls or baseboards).

The average walk-through takes about 90 minutes, after which the builder and you can sit in the kitchen and review the punch list again and determine a reasonable schedule. At some point, the builder will ask you to sign off on the condition of the house and your satisfaction of its quality and workmanship.

Final Inspection and CO

Assuming there is a local building department or regional authority that issued you a permit and has been inspecting your home during construction, your vacation home will require a final inspection (or a "final" in builder lingo). The final inspection is commonly routine, but not necessarily a cakewalk; primarily, the inspector will verify previous inspections have been made (and passed) and generally ensuring that the house is ready for occupancy.

On final, the inspector will test all of the mechanical, plumbing and electrical systems (specifically the service boxes and any complex schemes), inspect and verify the design of any staircases and handrails and examine the ventilation systems, among other health and safety items as specified in the building code.

He or she also will make sure that all floors are finished, light and plumbing fixtures have been installed and that the vent registers and faceplates are attached. If there are any missing items related to the building code, or which may endanger an occupant, the inspector won't

A vacation home should be designed, built and finished with several rooms that inspire relaxation, comfort and connection to nature.

approve the house for occupancy and must be called back when those items are in place or remedied.

Building codes are written and enforced to set the minimum standards for health and safety and have nothing to do with workmanship beyond any issue that might pose a hazard. A "code-compliant" house may be well built, but the two terms are not synonymous. For instance, an inspector won't comment on a gap between the wall and cabinets, or a poor trim job. That'll be your job when you tour the house with your builder, called a walk-through (see above).

In addition to a final inspection, you may also need an improvement survey, which will document the actual placement and dimensions of your vacation home on its site and list other elements (property lines, rights of way, landscap-

Building codes are written and enforced to set the minimum standards for health and safety and have nothing to do with workmanship.

169

ing) related to the house and its now-improved lot. The improvement survey, conducted and documented by a surveyor, may be a part of the necessary paperwork to gain a Certificate of Occupancy and/or legal transfer of the title.

Once the house has passed final inspection, your builder should then submit the completed inspection card (or set of cards, plus any other required documents) back to the building department for a Certificate of Occupancy. Upon your receipt of the CO, the process of transferring title and closing escrow can occur.

Maintenance and Caretaking

For a vacation home, maintenance and caretaking are critical considerations given your occasional or seasonal use of the house. Unlike with your primary residence, you won't be able to trim the hedges or rake the leaves—or any of the ad-hoc chores you now do around the house that make it looked lived-in and cared for.

Preparation during the spring and summer months, such as making repairs to the roof and siding, can mitigate winter maintenance tasks.

Photo courtesy Town & Country Cedar Homes

The design and construction of your second home should have addressed the performance and durability of exterior finishes, windows, doors and other components exposed to the elements, with a compatible consideration for easy maintenance of those products and systems when you make your weekend visits during the year.

More crucial is the caretaking aspect—of maintaining the yard and grounds, watchdogging potential problems and hazards due to extreme weather conditions (such as a heavy snowfall or high winds)—items and issues you'll be mostly blind to from your primary residence.

Ideally, a vacation home allows you to relax and enjoy activities inside the house and easily take advantage of your favorite outdoor amenities, as well.

For the most part, vacation homeowners do nothing; some have the advantage of having built their second home in a managed subdivision or resort area that provides (for a fee) caretaking and security services. If such services are not an option for you, consider hiring a local caretaker, either a real estate agent, property manager or other trusted company or person, to keep an eye on your place when you're not there.

It is ultimately your responsibility to care for and maintain your second home.

The cost of a caretaker is minimal, perhaps $50 per month or less depending on the scope of their responsibilities—well worth it to make sure your vacation retreat is safe and secure, and to ensure you are quickly informed of any problems or issues that arise when you're away.

That said, it is ultimately your responsibility to care for and maintain your second home. Help yourself by following a year-round maintenance schedule, which may include such tasks as changing the furnace filter every three months, keeping debris off the roof, redirecting the downspouts and splash blocks away from the foundation and keeping the gutters clean. Also, keep a set of basic carpentry and yard tools at the vacation house so that you (or your caretaker) can easily and quickly fix minor problems on the spot.

Relaxing on a back porch with a view of the ocean, mountains or lake is often the ideal activity for vacation homeowners — and the ultimate reward for a job well done.

Enjoying Your Home

As you finish this book, either as the first step on the road to creating and building a vacation home, or as you actually follow that process, the most tangible benefit of your hard work, research, preparation and execution will be the first time you open the door to your vacation retreat and enjoy a long weekend away from home.

Photo courtesy Precision Craft Log Structures

No matter what you plan to do in your new vacation getaway, from outdoor recreational activities to lounging on the couch with a good book, you'll no doubt take comfort in the fact that the house you're in is yours, by your design initiative and careful planning. It is, in fact, your reward—one that you can enjoy for many, many years to come.

Glossary of Terms

2-by/4-by—the nominal size, in inches, of the narrow plane of standard wood framing components, as in a 2-by-4.

allowances (code and budget)—in the building code, the acceptance of similar, if not exact, provisions that meet the code; in budget terms, an amount of money provided to the buyer for the purchase of certain items or products of their choice, such as appliances and light fixtures.

chase—a space or area in the structural frame provided for ductwork and other utility conduits to hide them from view.

cladding—a covering over a lesser-grade or vulnerable structure or material, such as a vinyl cladding over a wood-sash window.

close of escrow—settlement of the deed; when title and deed to the house and property are transferred from the seller (the builder) to the buyer or homeowner after certain legal and financial conditions are met.

CMUs—industry abbreviation for concrete masonry units, or concrete blocks.

codes—standards of practice and design enforced by the local building department to help ensure basic health and safety provisions and other protective measures.

combustion appliance—natural gas-operated appliances or equipment that rely on combustion air to fuel (or allow to burn) the natural gas.

concrete pour or "the pour"—the process of literally pouring wet concrete into the forms or other mold.

condensation—the formation of water from airborne moisture on a surface when the temperature of that surface is below that of the air.

conduit—a hollow gateway, typically a length of pipe that carries and protects wires, water or other utility.

covenants—the rules of a community governing such things as landscape design, features and maintenance, house color and other items that impact the overall value of the neighborhood or community.

cut-off date—the last day a change can be made or a product ordered without incurring extra cost or delaying construction.

cured—dry, as with concrete or mortar.

drywall—sheets or panels of pressed gypsum encased in paper; used to create interior wall surfaces.

duct—the conduit through which forced air (heated, cooled or exhausted) is delivered.

ductwork—the series of ducts leading to and from the furnace or other heating or cooling equipment throughout the house.

eaves—the bottom edges or other portions of the roof that extend beyond the outside walls of the house.

elevation renderings—realistic and to-scale line drawings of the home's exterior, as viewed from ground level.

engineered wood—structural and non-structural lumber that is made by reconstituting wood fibers, mixing them with resins and other adhesives and forming them into dimensional lumber as alternatives to milled or solid-sawn lumber.

faceplate—a plastic or metal plate that fits over an electrical outlet or switch to protect and cover the wiring.

fixture—a product fixed to the structure, most commonly regarding plumbing products such as toilets, tubs and sinks, or lighting, such as in a ceiling.

flashing—protection against water or moisture infiltration, typically around roof protrusions and windows.

floor joists—framing components that create the structure of the floor.

footings—the part or section of the foundation that transfers and spreads the weight of the structure to the soil.

forms/formwork—the molds into which concrete is poured to form walls, slabs and footings.

framing crew—the group of workers hired to build the home's structural frame.

freeze-thaw cycles—the systematic freezing and thawing of elements or products, such as plumbing pipes, which may result in damage or failure.

frost line—the depth at which the ground freezes in your area.

gas line—the pipe that delivers natural gas or propane to an appliance.

GFI/ground fault interrupter—a device that ensures grounding of the wire to protect against electrical shock or short circuits.

grade—ground level, either natural or cut.

ground water—an underground source of water; an aquifer (as opposed to surface water, such as a reservoir).

humidity—the amount of moisture in the air.

HVAC — refers to heating, ventilation and air conditioning systems of a home.

in-house crew—workers on the builder's payroll, as opposed to subcontractors.

lead times—the amount of time between ordering a product or material and when it is delivered.

load—the weight of a given component or area of a house.

load-bearing—a piece or section that supports weight from above.

lumber load—the lumber delivery to the job site.

mechanicals—a broad term referring to the plumbing, electrical, heating and cooling and other utility-driven operating systems in the house; specifically, may be used as synonym for the HVAC systems only.

mortar—a mixture of concrete paste and aggregate (rock or minerals) used to connect or secure ceramic or stone tiles to a surface.

pad—a developed piece of ground, or lot, upon which the house will be built.

panelized wall sections—sections of framed walls built in a factory and delivered to the job site.

parcel—a piece or section of land, typically undeveloped or unimproved but designated for a certain type of building or other development.

planned development—a subdivision or newly constructed neighborhood of homes, starting with an undeveloped or unused section of land.

pitch—the angle or slope of the roof.

pre-built components—sections of a house frame or structure built in a factory and delivered to the job site, such as plated roof trusses and panelized wall sections.

rafters—a series of sloping, parallel structural framing members that form the shape of the roof.

rebar—reinforced steel bars set in wet concrete to add strength and stability.

roof trusses—pre-assembled sections that form the shape and structure of the roof.

setbacks—the distance from the property or lot lines to the actual structure (all sides), as determined by local zoning ordinances. Setbacks determine or regulate the space between neighboring homes.

set the forms—the process of building and reinforcing the formwork or forms in preparation for concrete.

Sheetrock—a brand name for drywall manufactured by United States Gypsum (USG) Corporation.

single-family housing—a structure or dwelling unit built for one family, as opposed to an apartment building or duplex.

site superintendent—the builder's representative during actual construction, in charge of the job site. The superintendent (also called supervisor or foreman) is responsible for managing subcontractors, materials delivery and maintaining the schedule, budget and quality of the project.

spotting a fixture—marking the location of or installing a product that is fixed to the structure.

sound abatement—the reduction of sound waves through a structure.

stick-framing—industry term for platform framing, with "sticks" being the individual pieces of wood or steel used to assemble the structural frame.

stubbed up—pipes or other utility conduits extending from the ground vertically and capped, which will eventually be connected to the home's various energy and water systems.

stucco—A cement plaster applied to the exterior wall or surface of a building as a finish.

subfloor sheathing—panels of plywood used on top of the floor joists to stabilize and enclose the floor structure, creating a flat platform.

subs—subcontractors, also known as specialty or trade contractors, such as electricians, plumbers, framers and painters.

tract housing—mass-produced housing, typically in a subdivision or other planned housing development.

the trades—subcontractors or specialty contractors, such as electricians, plumbers and painters.

value-engineering—the process of evaluating the cost and structural value of a product or material to the overall structure.

vaulted ceilings—angled or pitched ceilings, as opposed to flat.

walk-through—a buyer's tour and inspection of the house, typically occurring upon the completion of the home.

wall cavity—the space between two wall studs.

water table—the topmost level of ground water or an underground aquifer.

RESOURCES AND BIBLIOGRAPHY

American Institute of Architects (AIA)
1735 New York Ave., NW
Washington, D.C. 20006
Phone: 202-626-7300
Web: www.aiaonline.com

Log Homes Council
National Association of Home Builders
(NAHB)
1201 15th St., NW
Washington, D.C. 20005
800-368-5242 or 202-822-0200 (in D.C.)
Web: www.nahb.com

American Institute of Building Design (AIBD)
2505 Main St., Suite 209B
Stratford, Connecticut 06615
Phone: 800-366-2423
Web: www.aibd.org

American Resort Development Assn. (ARDA)
1220 L St., NW, Suite 500
Washington, D.C. 20005-4018
Phone: 202-371-6700
Web: www.arda.org

The Home Building Process: Everything You Need to Know to Work with Contractors and Subcontractors, by Rich Binsacca; 2000, Home Planners, LLC, Tucson, Arizona; ISBN: 1-881955-63-X.

Everything You Must Know When Building Your Country Home, by Homer Emery, Ph.D.; 2000, Home Planners, LLC, Tucson, Arizona; ISBN: 1-881955-71-0.

Vacation & Second Homes (home plans book); 1999, Home Planners, LLC, Tucson, Arizona.; ISBN: 1-881955-57-5.

Waterfront Homes (home plans book); 1999, Home Planners, LLC, Tucson, Arizona; ISBN: 1-881955-64-8.

Guide to Buying a Second Home for Vacation, Retirement, Investment and More!, by Ruth Rejnis, et. al.; 1998, Dearborn Financial Publishing, Inc., Chicago, Illinois; ISBN: 0-7931-2711-4.

Buying Your Vacation Home for Fun & Profit, by Ruth Rejnis and Claire Walter; 1996, Dearborn Financial Publishing, Inc., Chicago, Illinois; ISBN: 0-7931-1583-3.

How to Find Your Ideal Country Home, a Comprehensive Guide, by Gene GeRue; 1994; Warner Books, New York, New York; ISBN: 0-466-67454-0.

Finding and Buying Your Place in the Country, 4th Edition, by Les Scher and Carol Scher; 1996, Dearborn Financial Publishing, Inc., Chicago, Illinois; ISBN: 0-7931-1785-2.

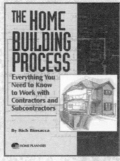

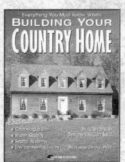

Rich Binsacca

About the Author

Rich Binsacca is a nationally award-winning real estate journalist, editor and author. His experience in home building includes stints as a laborer for a small remodeling firm and as the project manager for a general contractor. In addition, he has served as an editor, reporter and/or contributor to such magazines as *Builder, Architectural Record, residential architect, The Practical Homeowner,* and *Custom Home,* among several others.

Rich also has written two other books on the subject of home building and real estate, most recently *The Home Building Process: Everything You Need to Know About Working with Contractors and Subcontractors,* published in 2000. He also co-wrote *About Your House with Bob Yapp,* a companion publication to the nationally syndicated PBS television series of the same name.

He currently resides in Boise, Idaho, with his two sons, Samuel and Nicholas, and their cat, Stripes.